# ACCELERAT~~ING~~

# PROJECT

# MANAGEMENT

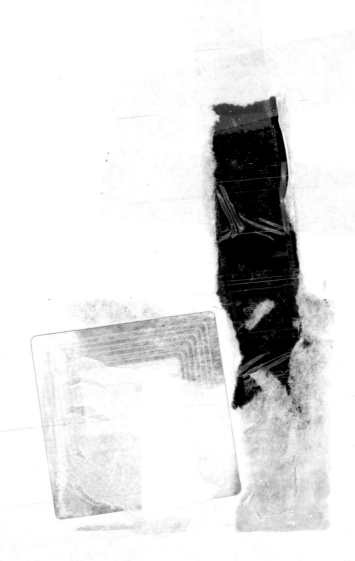

# ACCELERATED PROJECT MANAGEMENT
## How to Be the First to Market

**JAMES P. LEWIS**

**LOUIS WONG**

McGraw-Hill

New York    Chicago    San Francisco    Lisbon    London
Madrid    Mexico City    Milan    New Delhi    San Juan
Seoul    Singapore    Sydney    Toronto

1 2 3 4 5 6 7 8 9 0 FGR/FGR 0 9 8 7 6 5 4

ISBN 0-07-142324-9

The Lewis Method is a registered trademark of The Lewis Institute, Inc. PMI and PMBOK are registered trademarks of Project Management Institute, Inc. PMP is a registered certification mark of Project Management Institute, Inc.

McGraw-Hill books are available at special quantity discounts to use as premiums and sales promotions, or for use in corporate training programs. For more information, please write to the Director of Special Sales, McGraw-Hill, Professional Publishing, 2 Penn Plaza, New York, NY 10121-2298. Or contact your local bookstore.

Library of Congress Cataloging-in-Publication Data

Lewis, James P.
  Accelerated project management : how to be the first to market / by James P. Lewis and Louis Wong.
      p. cm.
  ISBN 0-07-142324-9 (pbk. : alk. paper)
  1.  Project management. 2.  Time management. 3.  New products—Management.
I. Wong, Louis. II. Title.
  HD69.P75L487 2004
  658.4'04—dc22

                                                           2004012343

# CONTENTS

**Chapter 9**

# Manufacturing: Turning a Sample into a Product    143

**Chapter 10**

# Competence Building through Learning    159

# PREFACE

One common theme pervades organizations around the world today: the need for speed. Alvin Toffler wrote presciently about the pervasiveness of change and pointed out that it was accelerating. And Tom Peters has said that "speed is life" and that organizations must "get fast or go broke."

This is especially true when it comes to developing new products. A general axiom is that the first company to introduce a new product to the market gains 70 to 80 percent of market share, and it is very difficult for subsequent entries to unseat the first-to-market. This fact alone makes Peters' comment highly relevant.

There are two ways to accelerate work. One is to change the process by which work is done—adopting a faster one, of course. A simple example is switching from a paintbrush to a roller. The second way is eliminate factors that cause work to slow. The most common cause of slowness is errors that are made, that then must be reworked. Improving quality of work increases speed.

The processes for developing products are largely technical, and they must be improved. We understand this. What we don't seem to understand is that the management of the development project can contribute as much or more to speed. Poor planning has been found to be one of the major causes of rework in projects. As fantastic as it may sound, there are cases of products being developed and turned over to manufacturing without any attention devoted to, say, designing a shipping container ahead of time; the time later required to design and acquire an appropriate container became a major holdup in shipping the final product. Proper project planning would have prevented such an event. This book addresses the project management aspects of developing products, not the engineering or technical aspects, although we do discuss the organization structures that contribute to speed and recommend those that have been found to help.

Louis Wong and I met in Singapore in August 2002. I was there to teach a project management seminar for the Singapore chapter of the Project Management Institute. He suggested this book, and I heartily agreed that there is a great need for it. We later discovered that we are both advocates of the Crosby method of quality improvement, and you will find discussions of some of Crosby's methods in these pages. Phil Crosby, who coined the term *zero defects*, was vice president of quality when I worked at ITT Telecommunications, and when I took a position as quality manager, following 12 years in product development, I was indoctrinated in his philosophy.

Louis was a quality manager at Philips. They embraced Crosby's methods, so he also became a disciple of the Crosby philosophy. We both strongly believe that improving quality of product development will contribute significantly to speeding up the process. As Crosby demonstrated, prevention of errors will ultimately reduce the cost of appraisal and failure costs in organizations, and project management can properly be thought of as a way of preventing errors.

We do assume that readers understand the essentials of project management, such as schedules and work breakdown structures. If this is not the case, you will find that two of my books offer a good treatment of the subject. These are *Project Planning, Scheduling, and Control* (Lewis, 2000) and *Fundamentals of Project Management* (Lewis, 2001).

We do like to hear from our readers. You can contact me at jlewis@lewisinstitute.com and Louis at louis_wong @ctl.creative.com.

Good luck with your projects!

**James P. Lewis**
**Vinton, Virginia**

**Louis Wong**
**Singapore**

# ACCELERATED PROJECT MANAGEMENT

# 1

## CHAPTER

# The Product Development Race

*If the '80s were all about quality, and the '90s were about re-engineering, the 2000s will be about velocity.*

— Bill Gates, Microsoft

The speed of bringing new products to market is no doubt one of the single most important factors that will determine the success or failure of a company. At one time, Hewlett Packard (HP) took 54 months to develop a new computer printer. This was reduced to 22 months to develop its first inkjet printer, and then 10 months for its first color DeskJet printer. Intel has reduced the time to introduce a new personal computer motherboard from 12 months to only 6 months (Smith & Reinertsen, 1995, p. 3). No matter how good your products are, if you introduce them to the market later

*Speed is one of the only competitive advantages you have.*

than your competitors, you won't be able to demand a premium price, and in many cases it is one of the most common factors that cause the downfall of a product. Therefore, being first to market and frequently introducing new models will obviously lead to the domination of a particular product family in this digital world. Studies show that the first product in the market will gain about 60 to 70 percent market share. Due to today's rate of change, if you take too long to finish a new product, it may just become obsolete. Speed is one of the few competitive advantages you have.

A study by HP showed that when they were a month late to introduce a new computer to the market, they would lose about one-third of the total product sales—which would eliminate any profit for that product. They also found that they could actually

**Speed is life!**

spend up to 25 percent more than originally budgeted to develop the product, and it would only affect profits by a few percentage points, *so long as they met the target market introduc-*

*tion date!* In other words, speed is more important than development cost in this market. Another example is the introduction of new handheld computers. In early 2000, HP introduced Jornada, which came with a black-and-white screen, compared to Compaq's iPaq, which had a brighter, color screen, a faster processor, and better performance (this was before HP bought Compaq). But at the end of year, HP had sold 350,000 units more than Compaq, which had sold only 90,000 units in the same year. The main reason: Jornada was introduced six months ahead of iPaq.

Let's look at a typical cash flow in a product life cycle, shown in Figure 1.1. A product development project usually starts at the concept and planning stage. At that time, most of the spending is applied to the feasibility study of a product, the study, and some mock-ups. These are only small investments. Once the project is approved, it enters the implementation stage, where the bulk of your investment is spent. These expenditures include (but are not limited to) equipment and production setup costs, prototype sample build (which normally are more expensive than the high-volume production build), the ordering of materials, the testing and evaluation cost of the new products, and the qualification cost (both internal and by customer). The product will start to generate income only when it enters the *mass production stage*, when you start to sell the product in quantity. Note that the money spent before the product is produced in quantity is your total investment. This is represented by area A in the diagram. When you have sold enough product to recover that investment (area B in the diagram), you have reached the break-even point. All revenue received to the right side of this point contributes directly to profit. The final point on the diagram is the extinction of the product, its end-of-life. At this point, you stop production, scrap any unused raw materials on hand, and set aside replacement parts to service units already sold. The longer the mass production stage, the bigger the sales quantity, and the bigger the profit.

**F I G U R E  1.1**

Cash Flow Analysis of a Product Life Cycle

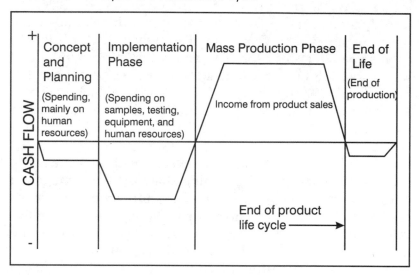

When we look at the cumulative cash flow (Figure 1.2), the maximum risk is prior to production, when you have invested in the production equipment and started to bring in raw materials for production. When the production quantity increases, the new product development project is now ready to enter its *closeout stage*. However, the product has not yet achieved *breakeven*. The breakeven point for the product is in the middle of the mass production stage, after the product has generated enough income to cover the total development cost. At this point there is not much the project team can do except to change the cash flow conditions.

However, the cash flow conditions can be greatly improved if the project is completed earlier. This is shown in Figure 1.3. When the development cycle is shorter, the new product is introduced to market earlier, the product price can be higher, and the production quantity will be greater: that means more market share and more profit. Furthermore, the

Cumulative Cash Flow over a Product Life Cycle

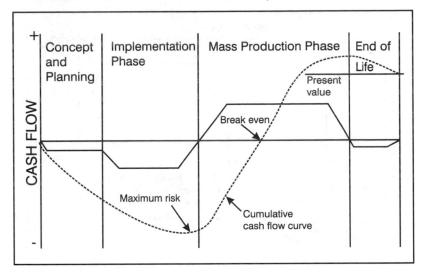

breakeven point will be earlier. Under these conditions, due to the shorter development cycle, the project team will have a better project focus, which will result in a higher "hit rate" (the project is more likely to achieve all its targets).

Thus, a shorter development cycle will lead to a number of financial benefits, such as lower risk, better cash flow control, an earlier breakeven point, and higher ROI (Figure 1.4).

The benefits of reducing the development time are obvious. In their book, *Developing Products in Half the Time*, Smith and Reinertsen (1995) suggest that early new product introduction not only enhances the pricing position for the product and increases market share, but also creates additional cost advantages as a result of the early manufacturing learning curve. Because of this learning curve, production can begin efforts for continuous improvement before the competition, which also leads to higher profits (Figure 1.5).

**F I G U R E  1.3**

Cash Flow for Reduced Development Time

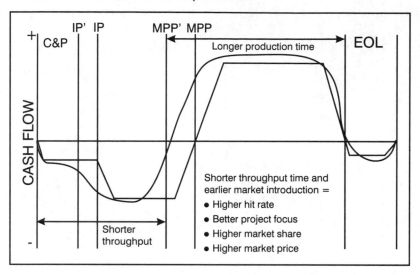

Product price inevitably must be reduced because of competition, so the earlier you introduce a product compared to your competitors, the easier it is to lower your production cost and maintain your profit margin. This is a big advantage. On the other hand, if you enter the market late, you have to lower your price to gain market share, but when your competitors lower their price in response, you will have little room to maneuver.

> One way to reduce the development cycle is through effective project management.

## THE NEED FOR EFFECTIVE PROJECT MANAGEMENT

Many companies have found that adopting sound project management methods allows them to introduce products

## F I G U R E  1.4

### Financial Benefits of a Reduced Development Cycle

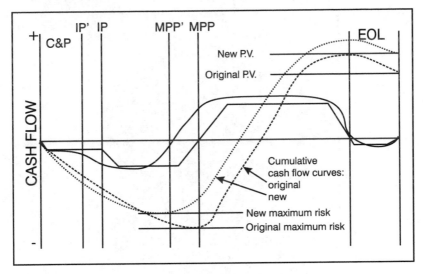

## F I G U R E  1.5

### Advantage of Early Product Introduction

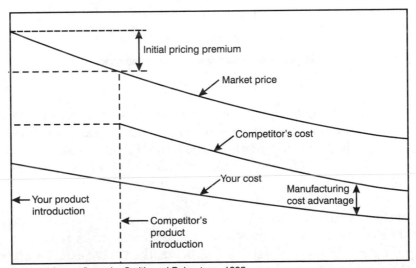

Adapted from a figure by Smith and Reinertsen, 1995.

*Adopting a good project
management method
helps ensure success.*

faster than their competitors. Formal project management becomes a standard way of working, where innovation and
new product development are the primary activities.

However, few companies consistently produce good results. Many of them have won the race for one or two products but were soon left behind in other areas. To be successful
in the new digital race, where product life cycles have become
shorter and product families are quickly replaced by new technologies, companies need to organize themselves differently
than in the '80s and ''90s. To consistently be first-to-market

(FTM), a company must establish an environment for *total project management,* which includes developing business processes that will foster the success of project management.

Successful projects depend on more than just improving project execution. Both internal and external factors influence a project, and many are beyond the control of the project team. Studies have found that the most common causes of project failure are:

1. Frequent change of specifications/ project scope.
2. Unclear project goals.
3. Unclear roles and responsibilities.
4. Inadequate estimation of required human resources and efforts.
5. Inadequate project monitoring and control.
6. Inadequate project management skills.
7. Inadequate risk management.
8. Poor project planning.
9. Staff turnover that affects the project.

## ROLE OF SENIOR MANAGEMENT

These factors must be addressed if formal project management is to succeed. The role of senior management is to create the best possible conditions for projects to succeed. To win in this lightning fast digital race, you must set your direction; start with formulating your vision for the company. The

> Senior managers must create the conditions needed for projects to succeed.

vision should establish the strategic direction of the company for years to come. It will allow you to decide which market you wish to conquer and to develop your long-term product strategy to dominate this market. Your team will turn your clearly defined strategy into an actionable product roadmap, and new product projects will then be realized through the *new product introduction process*, and its supporting processes, the *platform and building blocks development processes*. In addition to these internal business processes, it is also important that you develop strong cooperation with your key component suppliers in developing new key components or new technology (this is called the *early supplier involvement process*). The strong link between product, production processes, and equipment architecture will enable you to ramp up your new products in a fast and reliable manner. Again, the tactic is not just improving project execution, as many books have suggested, but also to create best processes and an environment in which project teams can excel.

So what are the optimal conditions for the project team? This is a difficult question. It depends on the maturity of the organization itself. However, it covers the following general areas:

1. Management's attitude towards projects.
2. A clearly defined product strategy and roadmap.
3. Critical component planning and development (external and internal).
4. Right-on-time projects, commitment-based project planning.
5. Systematic project management organization structure.
6. Resources planning and competence building.

## 1. Management's Attitude toward Projects

One day after the company's strategic product planning meeting, the project management office (PMO) manager asked the general manager, "Since we have set priorities for the top six projects in the company, and have allocated resources accordingly, I suggest we cancel the six nonpriority projects still on the priority project list. These projects are not critical to our product roadmap, nor have they received any firm project commitment from the project managers. Hence we should cancel them so that the project teams have a clear direction." The general manager replied, "Oh no, let's just leave them on the priority list. The engineers can just do these projects in their spare time. Maybe we just do not push them to complete projects per the project plan."

This is not a fabricated story. It happened. Senior managers are sometimes unaware of the implications of their decisions. If there is no clear direction on priority and importance of a project, the agreement to allocate resources by the next-level managers and the commitment by the project team members will never be secured. The end result may be devastating. You could guess that, after this conversation with the general manager, the projects did continue but none of the "priority projects" were completed on time, nor did any of the nonpriority projects ever get moving, as the general manager had wished.

Senior management's role in setting the right conditions for projects cannot be overstated. There are a few important tasks that senior managers cannot delegate to the next-level managers, and prioritizing projects so that they support the strategic direction for the company is one of them.

Following are the project responsibilities of senior management:

- **Project priority:** Define clearly the priorities of active projects and the top three to five *must-do* projects. This creates a sense of urgency and importance for the respective project teams and the whole company. However, don't overdo it. No organization can focus on more than five projects at the same time. Review and update your priority list at least every six to nine months.

- **Adequate resource allocation:** Allocate the resources and budget for each project. You do not expect free lunch in your business dealings, right? So you will have to invest your resources into the project before you can gain a profit in return.

- **Management milestone review and approval:** If you do not care, no one will. You must lead by demonstrating attention to the progress and success of the projects.
- **Approval of the alternatives:** When a project is in trouble, the team will come up with suggestions and an alternative plan. To show your support and endorsement of their actions, you must seriously review the alternative plan—and approve it if you agree with it.
- **Closeout of the project:** Time to assess and learn from the project—and ideally to celebrate success. This is a way of *encouraging the heart* (Kouzes & Posner, 2002) that motivates the team for future success.

Another important role for senior management is to state clearly what they want in the product roadmap. It is not uncommon in the middle of project execution for management to say, "We need these new features and functions to be included in this product. If we do not include them, we will not be able to sell it." While this may be true, management typically underestimates the degree of delay that such changes cause. Not only does the project team have to work on the new features and functions, but they also have to rework what they've already done. This will cause a longer delay than just adding in the new features and functions. More importantly, management has missed two important improvement opportunities:

1. To examine why these features and functions were not included in the product roadmap in the first place, and how to prevent this from happening again.
2. To discover the root cause of the project delay. Since there were many new requirements and features added along the way, there is no way the project team can know if the delay was due to the project team or to the additional new requirements.

There is often a disconnect between engineers and senior managers, which is illustrated by a story widely circulated over the Internet.

A man in a hot-air balloon realized he was lost. He reduced altitude and spotted a woman below. He descended a little and shouted, "Excuse me, can you help me? I promised a friend I would meet him an hour ago. I am late but I don't know where I am."

The woman below replied, "You're in a hot-air balloon hovering approximately 20 feet above the ground. You're between 40 and 41 degrees north latitude and between 59 and 60 degrees west longitude."

"You must be an engineer," said the balloonist.

"I am," replied the woman, "How did you know?"

"Well," answered the balloonist, "Everything you told me is technically correct, but I have no idea how to make use of your information, and the fact is I'm still lost. Frankly, you've not been much help at all. If anything, you've delayed my trip."

The woman below responded, "You must be in management."

"I am," replied the balloonist, "but how did you know?"

"Well," said the woman, "You don't know where you are or where you're going. You have risen to where you are due to a large quantity of hot air. You made a promise which you've no idea how to keep, and you expect people beneath you to solve your problems. The fact is you are in exactly the same position you were in before we met, but now, somehow, it's all my fault."

## 2. A Clearly Defined Product Strategy and Roadmap

Another key role for management is to set a clear product roadmap with specific key features and functions. This is very important, as the roadmap provides a clear direction for the project as well as the technological advancement required for future projects.

When a company lacks a clear strategy on the type of products it wants to produce, or its schedule to introduce new products, it becomes a follower of other companies or market leaders. This leads to poor product roadmaps and smothers the impetus for key technology breakthroughs. So the company lags in developing new technologies, or relies on cooperation with key suppliers to develop more cost-effective solutions. This leads to delayed product introduction and further losses to the competition. At the same time, the company is pressured to speed up project development. However, due to the delays, the project teams are forced to work on unrealistic project schedules. More short-cuts and trade-offs lead to more rework. This delays projects even further. As a result, projects are always late, and late-to-market becomes a norm. This leads to poor product strategy—and more poor product roadmaps. The whole vicious cycle starts again, a vicious cycle that only strong management determination and action can break.

## 3. Critical Component Planning and Development (External and Internal)

With a clear product roadmap, many of the key features and functions based on new technologies or new key components are now defined. This gives the team more time to prepare for the development of these components. While most companies prefer to develop new technologies and key components themselves, this may not be the optimal approach. To win the digital race, where technology change is swift and product life cycle is getting shorter, it is better to let the experts develop the new technologies while you leverage them to develop your products. However, this is easier said than done, especially if you have to cooperate with your key component supplier to define a future technology that is important to you but does not yet represent a clear market for your suppliers. Identify key suppliers who are willing to be your long-term partners to create a win-win situation. Developing a product internally is challenging, and developing a product with a supplier could be even more challenging because of different organization structures, culture, and approaches. To overcome these difficulties, a focused team will develop a technology roadmap with the commitment of its suppliers.

## 4. Right-on-time Projects

Big projects violate organizational physics (, 2002) Think about this: if you have 200 strong developers, do you want to commit to a two-year-long project that takes up more than 30 percent of your resources and have no deliverables until two years down the road? No project team can predict accurately much beyond 6 months. A project team in general is capable of listing all the tasks required for

> Nobody can see much beyond three to six months. Longer duration projects often get into trouble.

the next 3 to 6 months to accomplish the deliverables as committed. Anything more than 6 months will just be an educated guess. Anything beyond 12 months will be just a wild guess. Short projects (3 to 6 months) with value-added deliverables and clear quality requirements (for each deliverable) will help to ensure that the projects are accomplished right on time, every time.

This seems to be common sense. But, as Mark Twain once said, the problem with common sense is that it isn't common. Most people prefer big projects so that they will have a big forecasted profit. Big projects also make people feel important. The reality is that these big projects are seldom on time and the budget is almost always overrun. The biggest problem is that the completion of the project is only a best guess to which no one is ever seriously committed. No one can really tell you what must be done a year or two down the road. Especially when technology is changing daily, a long and/ or big project lacks

> The problem with common sense is that it isn't common.
>
> —Mark Twain

flexibility and can hardly be modified along the way. That is why some big, successful companies like CISCO have no projects longer than 90 days as a matter of policy.

This, however, does not mean that you do not have a clear product strategy for more than six months. What it really means is that you need to scope, manage, and prioritize your projects differently. You need to break big, long projects into smaller projects that have clear value-added deliverables. There are many advantages of this practice:

- Smaller projects take up fewer resources and are focused on the value-added deliverables.

- Due to the short lifespan, there is little or no chance for changing the specifications/requirements, which were determined and committed to up-front.

- The team is clear about the requirements and tasks necessary to complete the project and is therefore more committed to making the project successful.

- Overall product strategy can be made more flexible to combine the many value-added deliverables from the smaller projects into one product or several products to suit market needs, leading to a faster development cycle and time-to-market.

- As the duration is short and deliverables/objectives are clear, it is much easier to manage and reward the team. Thus team morale usually remains high.

## 5. Systematic Project Management Structure

With many smaller projects running at once, you need an overview of their progress. A management overview is essential for you to provide the support when needed and give a small push when projects lag. This is always part of senior management focus, especially when your company's future is heavily dependent on the success of these projects. The innovation project office (IPO) (in the United States this is commonly called simply the project office) will provide the metrics to monitor the health of the projects and acts as a key link between strategy and implementation. The IPO provides an early warning before the project veers out of control, and it looks for possible alternatives to make necessary adjustments. The IPO provides the following added-value services:

a. An overview of project progress
b. Project deliverables management (bridging the gap of the product roadmaps)
c. The reallocation of short-term development resources
d. Establishing and maintaining PM standards, methods, and templates
e. Turning lessons-learned in each project into knowledge for future projects
f. Providing project management training to improve the effectiveness of projects
g. Assessing project management maturity of the organization and executing improvement actions

## 6. Planning and Competence Building

While setting the conditions for your team to excel, you also want to set up the basic structure that will enable them to communicate, discuss, and resolve problems. The technical experts are always the most important and scarce resources in the company. Making the best use of this talent is the most difficult part of managing resources. Most organization structures are either full-functional or matrix (see Figure 1.6). These structures do not provide the best possible conditions to fully utilize scare resources.

In many companies, technical experts are tasked to head a functional department where half of their time (if not more) is spent in administrative paperwork. Nowadays, many successful companies have grouped all these functional experts as a "resource center" (Philips calls it the Innovation staff) with specific expertise (product development, process development, engineering, quality validation, logistics, cost calculation, etc). The project draws resources from the resource center, as defined by the project plan and schedule. The resource center is responsible for building up the technical competence of the Innovation staff and delivering the right technical solutions. Based on the long-term product roadmap, it also manages the department's capacity to meet long-term project requirements. Technical councils—e.g., quality council, software development council, etc.—are formed to align technical aspects of products and design principles, and to enforce basic design rules. Project managers are responsible for developing processes and integrating technical tools, such as FMEA, into project execution and control.

A resource center brings about a major change in the role of functional managers. It supplies professional engineers to work on the project. The process, integration of the roles for specific functions (such as quality and software development), project plan, and budget are the responsibilities of the project team. The quality engineer, for example, is responsible for carefully reviewing the quality requirements of the project and formulating actions to prevent problems. The quality engineers then prepare a quality plan for the project team to review. To support the quality engineers, there should be a quality council to provide technical expertise for issues that the engineer is not capable of handling, or that need a senior engineer's advice. Senior quality professionals

F I G U R E  1.6

Functional and Matrix Organization Structures

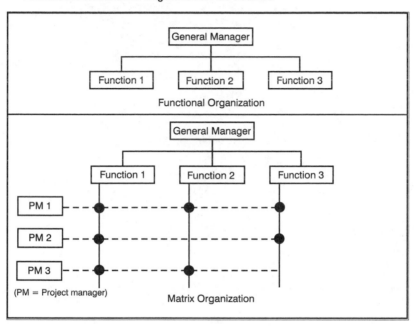

head the quality council, and this forms part of the resource center's plan to build up technical competence. However, the quality council should not be involved in the project directly, nor should it try to control or resolve specific project problems. The council reviews and challenges the design to ensure that design principles are sound and basic design rules are followed. As such, it remains accountable for the robustness of the technical solutions. The same approach applies to other disciplines as well. This has been found to be the best way to fully utilize experts in their respective specialized fields.

# 2
CHAPTER

# Management's Role: Creating Winning Conditions

*Leadership is ultimately about creating a way for people to contribute to making something extraordinary happen.*

— Alan Keith, Lucas Digital

There is a Bible story that has relevance for the management function in any organization. Jesus told of a farmer who went out to sow his seed. As he sowed, some seed fell on the path and was trampled, and the birds came and ate it. Other seed fell on rocky ground where there was very little soil. It sprang up at once because the soil was not deep. But when the sun rose, it scorched and withered for lack of roots. Some seed fell among thorns, and the thorns grew up and choked it. In the end, it produced no grain. And some seed fell on rich soil and produced a good crop.

Although this was not what Jesus was talking about, the sower can be compared to management, and the seed to the company's staff. It is management 's role to create the environment in which the seed can grow—that is, the staff can perform at its best. The seed that fell on the path is like staff that has no support or supervision. They are just left alone. They perform without passion. They feel they make little or no contribution to the company. They usually leave the company as soon as another opportunity comes along.

The seed that fell on rocky ground is like staff doing jobs that do not match their skills/capabilities or their expectations. They usually have no commitment to such jobs. Because of this, when they encounter some difficulty or setback, they either leave or get fired.

The seed that fell among the thorns is like staff that engages in office politics and infighting. They spend most of their time fighting with each other, trying to gain advantages over other functions, and thus produce few or no results for the company.

The seed that fell on rich soil represents staff that is highly productive because they flourish in a positive and constructive environment.

The moral of this interpretation is simple: the major responsibility for management is to create a positive environment for the team so that the team can be creative, cooperative, and confident that it can outperform competitors.

Just what is a positive environment for projects?

## THE POSITIVE PROJECT ENVIRONMENT

To answer this question, let's first look at the process of a development project and the role of management at each stage. In general, a project has five distinct stages:

1. **Concept stage:** At this stage, you conduct research on customer needs and study the feasibility of prod-

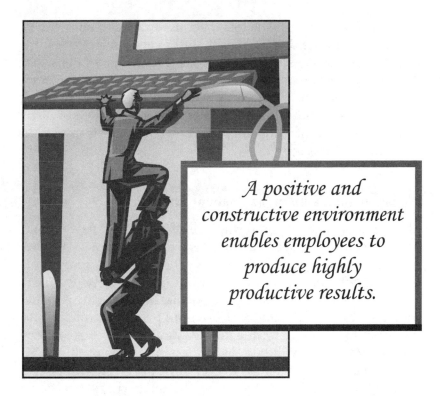

*A positive and constructive environment enables employees to produce highly productive results.*

ucts that will fulfill these needs. This includes a survey of competition.

2. **Definition stage:** Here you define the project scope, funding, product requirements, and time line. This includes risk analysis, considering potential problems and alternative plans, and compiling a complete team member list.

3. **Planning:** Formulate a plan to start, implement, and control the project, including risk management and contingency plans.

4. **Execution:** Implement the plan, monitor progress, and control for deviations.

5. **Closeout:** Draft final reports, lessons learned, and other reviews.

While it is unrealistic to expect the management team to be involved in the details of each and every project at its different project stages, there are some generic guidelines that the management team should apply to create a positive environment in which teams can operate to their full potential. Following is an outline of these key generic guidelines. (The technical details of managing a project will be discussed in the next few chapters.)

## Management's Role in the Concept Stage

The concept stage is the birthplace of a project, so it should be thoughtfully conceived, planned, and scheduled, following the overall product roadmap. There should be no surprises. Each new project should follow closely the new product introduction schedule as defined in the product roadmap, an action plan for the overall product strategy, and the company's vision for the future. Management's role at the concept stage is to validate the key assumptions of this product/project as they relate to overall product strategy and current market conditions. Based on the latest market research and other market intelligence, management can decide to give its blessing to start this project as planned, make some necessary adjustments, or abandon it if it is deemed unlikely to be viable in the market.

However, the most important role is to review and uncover information that ensures that the product roadmap will be more accurately prepared in the future. This is a process of learning and accumulating knowledge. Most companies do review the business case of a new product introduction project, but very few review the accuracy of the predictions for this project, as laid out in the roadmap, and learn from the experience. Since management envisions the future and provides a clear direction for the company, the accuracy of the product roadmap is most critical. If it is not clear and accurate, the company has no way to plan and organize projects, and this includes funding, human resource allocation, equipment allocation, and so on.

As mentioned in Chapter 1, an inaccurate product roadmap creates a vicious cycle that standardizes delays in new product introduction and is hard for management to break. In fact, the only way to break it is to continue to learn from mistakes made on previous projects—especially those of poor prediction—and hold product managers accountable for the accuracy of the roadmap.

Following are some key areas on which management should focus during the concept stage:

1. **Customer orientation:** Does this product/project focus on customer needs? What are the customer expectations for this product? How well does this product meet those expectations? How do our competitors address customer needs?

2. **Product roadmap accuracy:** How well is this product placed in the product roadmap? Are key features supported by the technology roadmap, and are these technologies now available and proven? What is the risk?

3. **Business case:** How well does this business case fit in the overall business strategy? Is this product/project in line with the overall company business strategy? If not, what are the key justifications to change the company direction/strategy?

4. **Resources:** Do the resources required agree with the allocations from the product roadmap? If not, what additional resources are required?

5. **Project manager:** Do you have the right project manager to manage this project?

6. **Learning:** A short lesson learned is done at each stage to capture what can be learned. What can be done to make the roadmap more accurate in its prediction?

## Management's Role in the Project Definition Stage

Once the management team endorses the project, a proper announcement should be made to inform all employees that the company will embark on this new project. This provides a clear sanction for the project team to function and a clear direction for the whole company. At this time, the project manager can finalize the scope of the project. This includes the function, features, and styling of the product. This is the most important stage for the project team, because many projects fail due to unclear requirements or frequent changes of specifications. Therefore, controlling product specifications and their changing scope is the project manager's most critical challenge.

Project managers are always under pressure to make changes in order to fulfill changing market conditions. Regardless of whether these changes are valid, they usually cause delays. Changes should be approved only if they are absolutely necessary in order to sell the product and marketing agrees to the delay. Alternatively, if a delay is unacceptable but changes are considered necessary, it is management's role to provide the resources needed to maintain the end date while accommodating the changes. However, in the case of a long-term project, it will be almost impossible to make changes and still release the product on time. This is one reason to favor shorter duration projects. Breaking a big project into smaller projects with clearly defined deliverables ensures that the project, once it starts, will be less likely to require any changes.

The key areas of management focus in this project definition stage are:

1.  **Project scope:** Are the project scope, and the product functions, features, and styling, defined and agreed upon? Do they match the requirements as defined in the roadmap?
2.  **Resources:** Are project human resources allocated according to plan? Any new requirements? Does the

*Funding and cash flow must be monitored and controled.*

allocation of resources cover all areas, including production operations/manufacturing?

3. **Budget:** Is this business case justified? What is the investment? What is the ROI? When is the breakeven point? What is the cash-flow schedule?

4. **Duration:** How long is this project expected to last? When will it be completed? When will the product be transferred to operations? What are operation's expectations on handover?

5. **Risk assessment and alternative plan:** What are the major risks of this project? What is its impact on other projects, and on the company? Any possible alternative plan? Did the project team review the

design rules and FMEA database to ensure that they learned from previous projects and will avoid the pitfalls and mistakes of those projects?

## Management's Role in the Project Planning Stage

The project planning stage is the very last step before the project enters the execution stage, but no project should launch without an agreed-upon project plan. We always say, "Fail to plan, plan to fail." This is especially true when an innovation team plans a new product development project without involving the operations team at the beginning, but hands over the product to them for mass production. From our experience, there are always disagreements at the handover stage. The project team wants to hand over the product to operations to begin mass production, but the operations will always say, "It's not good enough!"

The requirements for handover are specified during the project definition stage. Still, there will be many gray areas that lead to disagreement. An effective way to minimize this problem is for the whole team to contribute to a joint project plan. This approach produces a single project plan prepared by all the team members—but controlled by the project manager. Only a jointly produced project plan should be presented to management for approval/endorsement.

However, there will be always some reasons for lack of participation by operations. Sometimes it is due to lack of information or awareness of the new project. (A proper announcement will help!) Sometimes it is due to lack of resources (operations is too focused on day-to-day problems). Whatever the reason, management's role is to prevent lack of participation and enforce mutual agreement in the project planning stage.

The key areas of management focus in this stage are:

1. **Project plan coverage:** Does the project plan cover the entire project up to mass production, and

include technical documentation, packaging, and market introduction? Do all team members, including operations, commit to this project plan?

2. **Timing:** Does the project plan match the product introduction schedule, as defined in the product roadmap?

3. **Critical path:** What are the critical paths of this project? Is there any alternative or contingency plan in case the critical path slips?

4. **Disagreement:** Does any disagreement about the project plan exist?

In short, management's role is to create a "one-team, one objective" concept for the cross-functional team to achieve. The project planning stage is the prefect starting point. Management must cultivate this climate and take the lead in creating a "One Project Team" environment.

## Management's Role in the Project Execution Stage

For any project, the project team will spend at least 80 percent of their time implementing the plan. Management should not spend much time monitoring the project, as this is the role of the project manager. However, this doesn't mean that the management team should treat the project team like mushrooms—leave them alone, keep them in the dark, and feed them rubbish. But it does mean that the management team should empower the project team and appoint the right project manager to the job. Senior management should spend time on a project at this stage only to get progress updates, recognize team successes (even small ones, rather than waiting for something big—or worse, waiting until the whole project is completed), or provide additional support when the project is faltering or falling behind schedule.

Having said that, we assume that the management team has established a standard process for product development, with key project milestones defined. They only need to follow the project progress according to the milestones defined.

The project manager, on the other hand, should give an early warning to management if something has gone wrong and present the management team with an alternative plan or a new catch-up plan.

Another key success factor is to assign a senior management team member to sponsor the project and thus establish a direct communication link with the project manager. The management team member should keep in touch with the project manager and get frequent but informal updates. He or she should act as a sounding board for the project team in order to secure management's support or recognition. This also eliminates the time needed by the project team to prepare formal presentations on status or answer questions from managers who do not follow or understand the project's progress.

For any project to function properly, funding is an important factor. Funding and cash flow are a company's bloodline—they must be monitored and controlled. Having said this, there is a caution: While the control of project funding is important, a highly rigid system sometimes creates unnecessary delays and excessive constraints. It takes a lot of time for the project team to re-apply for funding during execution of the plan. In most cases, the existing financial system is unsuitable for project control. A project-focused organization should review and reorganize its financial control system to meet the needs of its projects.

When the business case of a new project is first presented, it should cover all major investments, including tooling, capital equipment, and facilities, together with the estimated schedule. Once it is approved at the concept stage, the project team then prepares a detailed cash flow schedule during the project planning stage. Once approved, this budget/cash flow schedule should be used as a baseline for the project team to follow. The project manager should be empowered to approve spending within this budget schedule.

The only time management attention and re-approval is required is when the spending will exceed more than 10 percent of its original commitment.

An update to the plan is only necessary if there are significant changes. The project team should be held accountable for the budget and cash flow, with the allowable deviation from target of +/– 10 percent. This system will empower the team to control its own budget and reduce any unnecessary control for cash flow while still providing the financial system with a clear and proper cash flow projection.

The key management focus at the project execution stage includes:

1. **Project progress against the committed milestone schedule:** Is the project team progressing according to the approved plan? Any major obstacles ahead? Will the project team be able to complete the project on time and on budget?

2. **Project human resources:** Have adequate resources been allocated? Any additional resources required?

3. **Project budget:** Is the project team spending within the approved budget? Any new funds required? Would any additional project spending accelerate the project so that it can be completed ahead of its original schedule? Would this investment be worthwhile?

4. **Recognize and celebrate even small successes:** Do not forget to reward the team and recognize even their small success. Remember that "success breeds success."

## Management's Role in the Project Closeout Stage

The happiest moment for a project team is definitely when it hands over a newly developed product to operations for mass production. This is the result of many months of hard labor by team members from different functions. At this project closeout stage, management should focus on two areas. One is the proper project handover to operations. Very often this is done in a very rushed manner. Operations personnel are often reluctant to accept responsibility for further product improvement, either in product quality or production yield improvement.

However, the management team should decide if the handover is valid in order to free up the development team to work on other projects. Management must maintain a balanced view and decide if the product being released is ready to start up production. Their second most important role is to ensure that the project team has learned from this project. The project team should present a formal lessons-learned report that documents the learning and improvement opportunities. These recommendations should turn into actions for future projects. These actions should also be translated into formal documents, such as design rules, and entered into the FMEA database for future reference.

One recommendation is that the project team should follow the product through the first production run and market launch. If there are problems encountered with the new release, they should be required to correct them. In this way, they will get immediate feedback on what they did—especially any errors that they made. This means that they cannot be allocated 100 percent to new projects until this stage has been completed.

The key management focus at the project closeout stage is on:

1. **Product handover:** Has the project team fulfilled all the handover requirements as specified in the project planning stage? Is the sustenance team (the group that will support the product once it is released) and its budget defined?

2. **What we have learned:** What are the major lessons learned? What was done well? How do we capture these activities in future projects? What needs to be improved in managing future projects?

3. **Celebration:** Remember to give due recognition to the project team and reward them accordingly.

## Management's Role in Office Politics

Edwards, Jr. said, "Environment is the overriding factor. What management perceived as the performance of the people is actually the efforts of people in the presence of the environment they work in. Management has to fix the environment, make it cooperative" (quoted by Kopelman, 2002). Whether you like it or not, office politics always intrude. In a project-oriented organization, the project manager must always spend time to fend off political attacks—both internally and externally—to keep the project on track. This is not to say that all office politics are bad. In some cases, they challenge the project team to do even better. However, excessive office politics hamper project progress and organizational growth. Management's role is to be aware of power plays and ensure that they are not destructive.

Office politics are here to stay, and as a leader you must be aware of the culture and political playing field in your company. Based on many studies of organizational dynamics (quoted by Christopher J. Harling, 2001), a company's personnel can be divided into four general groups:

"Lambs" represent those people who are honest and capable in their jobs but weak in playing politics. (Those who are not capable and are also weak in politics will never survive in the first place.)

"Wolves" represent those people who have better political skills than the lambs but are weak in completing their tasks. Wolves like to take credit from lambs, and they use their political skills to hide their incompetence.

"Foxes" represent those who have strong political skills and are also competent in their jobs, but who focus on their own gains. They manipulate the situation to advance themselves instead of the objectives of the company.

"Owls" represent the wise individuals who have the company's goals at heart and do everything possible to achieve these goals. They are both competent and diplomatic.

Your role as a leader in the organization is to unite the team to achieve a common goal, eliminate the wolves, and develop the lambs to become wise owls. The very first step is to minimize politics among the project teams. The teams must be able to operate in an open, honest environment so that they will channel all their energy to the project and technical problems. As director of Professional Development for the Project Management Institute's Singapore Chapter, this book's co-author, Louis Wong, has many opportunities to speak to project team leaders from different organizations, and they have commented that they (including their team members) spend as much as 20 to 60 percent of their time making presentations, attending meetings, and engaging in negotiations just to avoid these political minefields. Imagine that time being saved for more positive project work, and the increase in speed that can aid in completing a project if these negative influences are eliminated!

To minimize office politics, the management team must remain neutral. Decisions should be made based on facts and figures, not impressions. In organizations where whoever shouts loudest gets the attention, you can bet that the right things are not done in the long run. It is especially important that the management team serve as a role model and not play politics themselves. Actions should always be guided by company objectives and not individual egos (Collins, 2001). Open and honest communication, plus "management by walking around," will help the management team keep in touch with all staff at different levels, thus minimizing the political games in the company. Following are some specific suggestions:

1. **An open door policy:** Keep communications open to all at all times. All employees must be able to openly discuss with you any issues and problems encountered, without fear of reprisal.

2. **A direct communication channel with project teams:** As was stated earlier, it is essential for a management team member to act as a project sponsor. This allows that person to understand any problems when they develop and to be the advocate for the project team at the management level. This is critical for the project's success, because it helps to resolve many problems quickly.

3. **Facts-based management:** Management should always make decisions based on facts and figures. The team must be able to justify their case through test results and objective analysis. The team should also be held accountable for their actions and learn from their mistakes.

4. **Management by walking around (MBWA):** Many management gurus have suggested that the management team must know what is really going on in an organization, not just through reports but through direct observation and experience. Through walking around and talking to the people doing the jobs, the management team will see with their own eyes what is going on and feel first-hand the pulse of the organization. Furthermore, when the management team knows what is really going on, it will be more difficult for people to cover up problems and play politics.

# 3
CHAPTER

## Product Strategy: Turn Your Vision into an Action Plan

*Doing the right things is more important than doing things right.*

— Peter F. Drucker

The success of every organization depends in large part on how well senior managers are able to integrate mission, vision, values, and strategy into a project portfolio that meets the requirements of the marketplace. Although it seems obvious when stated, managers sometimes forget that it does no good to accelerate projects that were ill chosen in the first place. The only result such actions achieve is a more rapid failure!

> *Managers sometimes forget the fundamental question: "What is our business?"*

As Peter Drucker has emphasized so strongly, the first question that must be asked by any organization—whether for-profit or not-for-profit—is, What is our business? (Drucker, 1973). All too often, in their zeal to succeed, managers forget this fundamental question. They try to be everything to everyone, and end up confusing their customers. In his books on branding, Al Ries (1993, 2002) provides examples of successful companies that forgot who they were and lost their way. It remains to be seen if this will be true of Amazon.com. They were highly successful in establishing themselves as an online bookseller. Now they sell CDs, apparel, and electronics, trying to redefine themselves as a highly efficient online store where you can buy almost anything you want.

It is outside the scope of this book to go into detail about defining a mission and vision for your organization, but until

> It does no good to accelerate projects that are ill conceived in the first place!

you can express it in concise, clear language, you are not ready to start accelerating your projects. Thus the following overview.

## MISSION, VISION, AND STRATEGY

In over 25 years of working with organizations on their performance issues, I have found that many managers are not clear about the differences between mission, vision, strategy, tactics, and logistics, so before we go any further, let's clarify

> A company's vision can be thought of as its self-image.

these terms. A company's vision can be thought of as its self-image. Your personal self-image is how you see yourself, and how you think others see you. It is often a surprise to individuals to learn that others do not see them the same way that they see themselves. For example, you may think of yourself as warm and friendly, and learn that others see you as cold and impersonal. As another example, I am a fairly strong introvert, but people who attend my seminars don't believe this. They can't comprehend that so outgoing an individual in the seminar room can become a very quiet, reserved person outside of it.

In any case, let's say that a company's vision is what management *wants* the company to be, and how they want customers to see it. The mission of the organization is to achieve that vision—to take steps that will cause customers to see the company in the desired way.

Strategy is the overall approach that the company takes to achieve its mission. A couple of examples may help clarify this. Consider a company that aspires to be very large, because management believes this is necessary for its success. Growth can be accomplished a number of ways. One is to be very aggressive in developing new products that meet market needs, based on very good

> Strategy is the overall approach that the company takes to achieve its mission.

information about market requirements. Another way is to grow by acquiring other companies that fit within the family of products produced by the company.

One growth strategy that I have observed I have dubbed the *predatory* approach. For instance, a large drug chain goes into a market and either buys up existing small pharmacies or prices their own products so low that local stores are forced out of business. In another case, a very large camera store chain moved into an area, then approached a quite successful local store with the ultimatum that they could either sell their four locations to the chain or be run out of business. The local store sold out. (I don't approve of

> Tactics are those steps taken to implement strategy.

this strategy—I am simply describing it as an example.)

Tactics are steps taken to implement strategy. As an example, if you decide to grow by acquisition, you must arrange for financing your purchases, unless you have access to a lot of cash. Logistics has to do with supplying your employees with materials, equipment, and an adequate work environment so that they can perform as required. This is an area sometimes overlooked by managers. Let's see how all of these fit together in managing a product-development project.

## THE LEWIS METHOD FOR MANAGING PROJECTS

In order to make it easy for everyone to understand the steps involved in managing a project, I have developed a flow chart that shows the steps and the sequence in which they are taken. (You can download a free, color version of the chart from the web site, www.lewisinstitute.com.) The chart is shown in Figure 3.1.

As is shown by the chart, there are five processes involved in a project. These are initiation, planning, execution, control, and closeout. In the model you will see that planning is subdivided into planning strategy and implementation planning. Also, as part of final closeout, a lessons-learned review is held to aid improvement of future projects.

### Initiation

The most critical process is definition. It is here that the seeds of failure are sown in perhaps 80 percent of all projects. As a former NASA program manager has written, "The seeds of problems are laid down early. Initial planning is the most vital part of a project. The review of most failed projects or project problems indicates the disasters were well planned to happen from the start" (Madden, 1995, p. 2). As stated earlier in this chapter, it does no good to accelerate a project that is heading in the wrong direction. We will return to this theme later in the chapter. For now, we want to give a high-level overview of each process.

In the definition step, a project team must be very clear on exactly what they are going to do. If developing a product, exactly what kind of product? What are the specifications?

## F I G U R E  3.1

The Lewis Method for Managing Projects

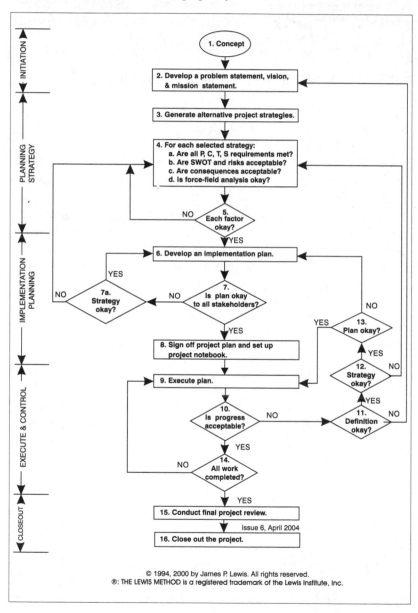

Who are the customers for the product, and what do they expect of it? These questions help the team clarify the vision—their mental picture of what the final result will look like, how it will perform, and so on. Unless there is a *shared understanding* of the vision among all team members, senior managers, marketing, and

> There must be a shared understanding of project vision, or problems will result.

other stakeholders, you can be sure that problems will result.

The mission of any project is always to achieve the vision, so a clear vision is the starting point. Once these two have been worked out—and only then—the team can turn to step three of the Lewis Method and discuss strategy.

## Planning Project Strategy

This part of project planning is often overlooked. It is assumed that the team knows how to go about the job without paying much attention to strategy. Or they simply fall back on a strategy that has been used in the past and been found to work. However, the old way is not necessarily the best way, so all possible strategies should be examined and the best one chosen for this particular project. We'll discuss how this is done later on.

## Implementation Planning

Once a project strategy has been chosen, tactics and logistics must be worked out. Exactly what steps must be taken to execute strategy? What kind of materials and equipment must everyone have in order to do their work? How long will each task take, in what order are they completed, and who will do them? How much will they cost? These kind of questions must be answered in this step.

## Execution and Control

Once a proper plan has been developed, work can begin. As the work is done, progress is monitored and compared to the plan. Are we where we are supposed to be? Are we on schedule, on budget? Is the performance of components under development acceptable? At any point where there is a deviation from plan, steps should be taken to get back on track. This is how control is exercised.

## Learning and Closeout

Once all work in the project has been completed, a lessons-learned review should be conducted by asking two questions. One is "What did we do well?" The second is, "What do we want to do better next time?" Notice that we don't ask, "What did we do wrong?" The reason is twofold—first, there is a possibility that nothing was done wrong, but we know that we can always do better next time. Secondly, people get defensive when you ask what they did wrong, and they tend to hide their mistakes. You can't learn from errors you don't know about, so it is a good idea to avoid any suggestion that people may be blamed or punished for errors they made.

## THE MODEL IN MORE DETAIL

Now that you have a general understanding of the model, we will move on to some more detailed comments. (This still will not cover the model in its entirety, since to do so would be to duplicate my book, *Project Planning, Scheduling, and Control,* 3rd Edition [Lewis, 2000]).

### Initiation

As stated earlier, this is actually the stage where many projects fail. Everyone assumes that they all understand and agree on project definition, vision, and mission, and this assumption simply proves to be incorrect.

I worked once with a team that had been given the job of cost-reducing a component used in an appliance. For nearly 10 years they had repeatedly refined the component, taking out 5 cents here and 25 cents there, until there was virtually no room left for further cost reduction. As we discussed the problem, it became clear that what was needed was a totally new concept for producing the component—not a rehash of the old design. They had already worked on the job for a couple of months before this realization occurred, and had struggled because no one could agree on exactly what they were trying to do. Yet they had begun the job believing that they were all in agreement.

This is so common that many stories exist about the failure of groups to manage agreement and disagreement. It is called the "false consensus" effect—the belief that everyone in a group agrees, when this is not true.

The important thing is to spend sufficient time discussing a project so that everyone can be certain that a true consensus exists. Note that not everyone needs to completely agree with the majority on the issue, but every member of the team must be able to say, "While I don't totally agree with all of you, I'm 100 percent willing to support the majority position." This is as close as you are likely to get to true consensus.

One point about mission statements. The mission of a team is *always* to achieve the vision. So vision must come first. What exactly is it that we are trying to produce? Once this question has been answered to everyone's satisfaction, the mission statement answers two questions:

1. What are we doing?
2. For whom are we doing it?

Answering "for whom" forces the team to think about the customer. Of course, there is some circularity in all of this because you can't define what you are doing unless you know your customer, so the mission statement simply reiterates what you already know.

## PROJECT STRATEGY

Note that this chapter is on *product* strategy, while this section is on *project* strategy. It is important that everyone understand the difference between these. Product strategy is the development of an approach to produce a mix of products that customers want and that gives the company a competitive advantage in the marketplace. Projects are conducted to develop products, and project strategy is the overall approach or game plan that will be employed to develop that product. We will discuss product strategy later in this chapter.

There are two possible kinds of strategies in a product development project. One is the overall project strategy. The second is the technical strategy. For simplicity, let's say that you must feed a group of people one evening. Asking yourself how you can do this, you arrive at the following possibilities:

1. Cook the food myself.
2. Take everyone to a restaurant.
3. Have the food prepared by a professional caterer.
4. Have a "pot luck" meal at which all guests bring a dish of some kind and share.

From this list of possible project strategies, the one that appeals to you is to cook the food at your home. You then consider how you will actually go about this, and five approaches seem possible:

1. Cook using a conventional range.
2. Have a backyard barbeque.
3. Microwave the food.
4. Have a fondue party.
5. Have a Chinese-style "hotpot" dinner.

From this list, you decide on a backyard barbeque. It will be fun. People can stand around the grill, even participate, and the weather is expected to be nice.

Then, the afternoon of the dinner, you get out your grill. The last time you used it was last fall; it is now May. To your dismay, the grill has developed rust, rendering it unusable, and you have no time to shop for a new one. What to do? Perhaps cook the food on the range? No, that won't be any fun. Fondue? No. Hotpot dinner? No. Microwave? Absolutely not.

This leaves no room for doing it yourself. There is no time for a caterer, and it is too late to tell people to bring their own food, so you are left with only one alternative—take everyone to a restaurant.

This example illustrates the fact that project and technical strategy interact. In product development, it may be that you want to employ a certain kind of technology, but you have no internal capability for it. You must either develop that capability or contract out that part of the project—or possibly abandon that particular technology.

An example of a change in technical strategy was the way in which Boeing designed the 777 aircraft. Previous designs were drawings done on paper. However, this two-dimensional approach almost always resulted in components inside the wing (for example) bumping into each other because they were located in the same place. This kind of interference is almost impossible to catch before a prototype is built, and then it is very expensive to correct.

The 777 was designed using three-dimensional computer modeling, so that such interferences could be seen on screen before any hardware was built; and, naturally, corrections could be made as well. Without a doubt, this saved Boeing a lot of money. It also saved time, because redesign eats away at a schedule.

It is important that a strategy (or combination of strategies) be chosen because it is the best one for this particular project, not just because "it represents how we have always done our projects." So in step three of the Lewis Method, you brainstorm a list of possible strategies, then pick one in step four. As you can see, you must ask several questions in step four, but, again, explaining how these questions are answered would be to duplicate my other book—so if you are interested, please refer to that. (Yes, this is a blatant attempt to get you to read my other books!) (Just joking.)

> A strategy should be chosen because it is the best one for the project, not just because it represents how the work has always been done.

## Implementation Planning

Once you have selected a strategy, you must develop a detailed plan on how to execute it. This plan will consist of a list of all tasks to be performed (called a work breakdown structure), a schedule showing task durations and sequencing, resource assignments, and a project budget. In most projects, the deadline is dictated. Your schedule must show how you will meet that deadline, or alternatively, what it is possible to do in the event that you have too few resources to meet the original target. Every project has four constraints—performance, cost, time, and scope (PCTS)—and because they are interrelated, trade-offs must be made. Three of them can have values assigned, but the fourth must be allowed to vary. In fact, one of the dozen or so most common causes of project failure is that the project sponsor dictates all four constraints.

> The people who will do the work should plan it!

One rule must be strictly followed in developing an implementation plan: The people who must do the work should prepare that part of the plan! This rule yields a double benefit. One is a realistic plan. The people doing the work have the best idea how long things will take and the order in which they must be done. The second benefit results from the first—because people put together their own plan, they are committed to it.

Implementation planning can take a lot of time, and one trap is for people to say, "We don't have time to plan—we must get the job done." This is actually counterintuitive. The more critical the time frame, the more important the plan becomes. It is when you have forever to get something done that the plan is unimportant.

## Execution and Control

Once work gets underway, control is exercised by comparing where you are to where the plan says you should be, and taking action to correct deviations that will inevitably occur. Since your plan tells you where you are supposed to be, it follows that if you have no plan, you have no control. This means

> If you have no plan, you have no control.

that planning is not merely an option if you want to actually control your projects.

Another essential aspect of control is that you can't have control if you don't know where you are. This is no trivial matter, especially in knowledge work. Attempting to measure progress in engineering, programming, science projects, or other knowledge work is virtually impossible if you try to do so using a continuous scale. That is, we can measure feet or meters on a continuous scale. We can measure time or volume on a continuous scale as well. But we can't measure work progress that way.

The best approach is to break knowledge work down into increments of one to three weeks' duration and measure two events—start and finish. It makes no sense to say a task is 60 percent complete, because you can't tell. In

> Development tasks should have durations not exceeding one to three weeks.

fact, you can't even be certain that some work is actually complete, but you are often forced to pretend that you can tell. Otherwise, you struggle forever attempting the impossible. Furthermore, by insisting that large tasks be divided into small ones with one- to three-week du-

## FIGURE 3.2

Progress Curve for Knowledge Work

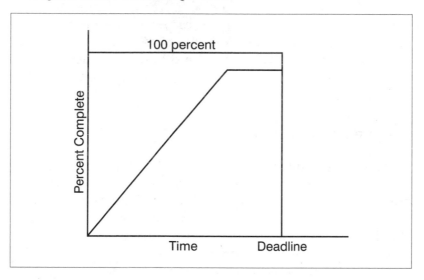

rations avoids the common problem in which a designer gets about 80 percent of the work done and then takes forever to complete the remaining 20 percent. The progress curve for such work is shown in Figure 3.2, and it is a universal curve.

## Learning and Closeout

One of the common mistakes teams make in projects is failing to do the lessons-learned review. Doing so most certainly means that mistakes made in one project will be repeated. Furthermore, the "good" things learned are not captured, so they cannot be employed in subsequent projects. Regular lessons-learned reviews should be part of every organization's culture, but not just at the project's end. The rule should be that these are conducted at major project milestones or every three months, whichever comes first. The reason for the three-month rule is that this is the limit of what people can reliably remember. The major milestone rule allows lessons-learned to be done on very short-duration projects before they are finished. The idea is to learn as you go, not just when the job is finished. The best examples of this being done correctly are in sports, where lessons-learned reviews are conducted after every game, and in the U.S. army, where such reviews are conducted after every simulation and every major battle.

## THE PROJECT PORTFOLIO

Developing products is always a gamble. You never know if you will sell enough to recover your investment, much less make a profit. The decision to develop a product is always based on guesswork. How much will it cost to manufacture? What will it cost to develop? How many units can we sell? What will customers pay for it?

There's a lot of witchcraft involved in answering these questions. In some companies you would be as well off examining the entrails of a dead chicken as you would believing the market forecasts or the estimates of development costs. In fact, I am almost convinced that this is how some companies do it. In one of my seminars I stated that many companies require a certain return on investment (ROI) before they will develop a product,

> Dividing one guess by another to get a magical thing called ROI is just a modern-day method of divining the future by reading the entrails of a chicken. It's just less messy!

and an engineer asked, "How do the marketing people determine how much it will cost to develop the product? They don't ask us engineers." I agreed with him. "In fact," I said, "they use sleight of hand. They begin with the ROI imposed on them by the company, and they forecast sales. Then they plug this into the equation and find out what the development cost must be to yield that ROI, and that is the number they use." We had a good laugh, and I know that not all marketing departments do this, but I have seen so many that do that it makes me wonder.

The fact is, in any case, that the market forecast is the best guess marketing has about sales, and even if engineering estimates development costs, that too is a *guess!* I know, I know: we would like to feel that there is some kind of precision in all this, but dividing one guess by another to determine a magical thing called ROI is just a modern-day method of divining the future by reading the entrails of a chicken. It's just less messy.

## Probability

In other words, all of this is probabilistic, not deterministic. There is a certain probability that you can sell the product. There is another probability that you can develop it for a certain cost, and another that it will cost a certain amount to manu-

> All estimating and forecasting is guessing!

facture. There are three important variables in product development, which I call the three Ps: performance, producibility, and profitability. The product must perform according to requirements. It must be producible in quantity. And it must be sold at a profit.

It is interesting that product developers often only understand one of these, performance. So long as they can make a product do what it is supposed to do, that's all they care about. It doesn't occur to them that it is unhelpful that they have made *one* unit work in the lab. They forget that the item must be made *in quantity* to be of value to the company. And of course, why make it in quantity if you can't sell it at a profit?

If all of this leaves you with a queasy stomach, it should. As I said, this is a messy business; essentially, it's gambling. The best thing you can do is to build a portfolio of products in which some are low-probability, high-payback; some are high-probability, moderate payback; and so on. Like investing in stocks, you need a proper mix for safety.

# 4
## CHAPTER

# Time Race:
# Right-on-Time Projects

*Hope is not a strategy!*

— Rick Page

## JIT PRODUCTION AND RIGHT-ON-TIME PROJECTS

We all recognize that the just-in-time (JIT) production strategy has changed the way that many manufacturing departments have been run since its transfer from Japan to the rest of the world around 1980. Many companies have also improved their productivity by focusing on quality improvement. As Phil Crosby has said, quality is free and is therefore profitable. There is a clear relationship between quality and productivity. When we improve quality, we also reduce cost and improve productivity. The JIT production system is considered the essence of an excellent production approach. JIT

*JIT attempts to eliminate waste.*

focuses on one very simple mind-set: Eliminate waste by having the right part, at the right place, at the right time.

The major aspects of a JIT system are:

1. Break a big production operation into smaller minicompanies and let each minicompany treat the next manufacturing process as their customer.
2. The teams manage the minicompanies. Each team has its own mission, goals, and targets, as well as its own performance indicators.
3. The teams will only provide "quality products" to their customers.
4. To achieve step three, the teams take quality very seriously. They will stop production immediately when they encounter a quality problem, and will only continue when it is fixed.

5. Teams meet regularly and track their own progress; review production processes and work on continuous improvements, report progress to management, and ask for help when needed.

6. A senior manager sponsors the minicompany, supporting and coaching it to ensure its success.

7. Management provides teams with training to enhance their problem-solving skills.

8. Teams are rewarded based on their results.

## Application to Projects

We can apply these simple JIT and quality concepts to project management. The fastest way to complete a project is to *do it right the first time*. If a project can achieve this, we call it a *right-on-time* project. Yes, it can be done—and it costs no more than doing it wrong. In fact, the cost to do it right the first time is zero! It will only cost you when you rework your project, and studies have found that nearly 30 percent of the cost of every project is rework. Clearly, we are not often enough doing it right the first time!

The basic right-on-time project concept is to focus on:

1. Eliminating causes of slowness.

2. Installing processes that accelerate project work and ensure that successes are repeatable.

## ELIMINATING CAUSES OF SLOWNESS

All project managers want to complete their projects on time and do the work right the first time, but few manage to achieve this goal. While a project manager may work hard to remove the roadblocks that slow down a project, he or she alone cannot remove all of these obstacles. To eliminate the root causes of slowness effectively, we must address them from a total system point of view. The management team must take the lead in resolving these problems. Experience

Take the lead in eliminating the root cause of slowness.

has shown that the following problems contribute to slowing down a project:

1.  The project is too big or the duration is too long.
2.  Project priorities are changed constantly.
3.  Too many product features.
4.  Not enough resources.
5.  Rework caused by poor quality.
6.  Poor planning, especially poor project definition.
7.  Perfectionism.

## Big Projects

Very large and/or long-duration projects almost always finish behind schedule. A big project with long duration (hereafter simply called a "big project") consumes most of an organization's resources, and does not provide a quick return on the investment. Worse still, because the market is often changing very fast, the new product's functions and features that were originally defined in the project scope may become obsolete because of competition. For a big project, you may have no choice but to change the project scope, to incorporate new functions and features in order to stay abreast of the competition. This will delay the project. Not only that, due to this changing project scope your project team will have to re-work what was done on the project and this will require more resources and funding.

Another problem with a big project is the changing of organization priorities. A project could be an important one in the beginning but if the project duration is long, it may become less important along the way, and very often some resources are pulled from one project to rescue another one. This action alone will delay the large project.

The positioning and scope of a product development project is a strategic decision made by senior management. In a fast-changing technology market, any new product development project must fit in a very small and narrow time-to-market window. As a result, new product development cycles are compressed. To compensate for this problem, you have to allocate more team members to the project, and the project team becomes very large. This leads to coordination and communication problems. The communication overhead alone is a very significant factor that can cause the project to proceed slowly. That is, the sheer amount of information that must flow between the project administrators and the team members can be overwhelming.

Another problem occurs when a company is not well prepared for a major technology change, and must develop a product with many new functions and features, incorporating these new cutting-edge technologies. Many of them are still under development and their results are not yet proven. The amount of risk incurred is significantly higher than that of a project that employs proven technology. Thus this type of project will often need a longer time to develop. All these factors contribute to the duration of a project. This is a major reason for trying to break large development projects into "bite-size" miniprojects, so that they can be completed in stages.

While a company may sometimes want to seize a new market opportunity by immediately creating a product to cater to its needs, it should not happen regularly. Pursuing projects that were not planned in the product roadmap is a reflection of poor market understanding, analysis, and forecasting. Management must address this critical problem as quickly as possible. Only when management has a full understanding of the market and is in control of the product introduction schedule can the size and scope of the project be planned and organized accordingly.

As a rule of thumb, a right-on-time project should not run longer than nine months, and the size of the full-time team should not exceed 10 percent of the company's development (innovation) resources. Smaller, short-duration projects are much more flexible than big projects; they have far fewer changes and are much easier for the team to grasp, plan, and execute. Thus, the chance for the team to accomplish the committed project targets is very high. The sole objective of right-on-time projects is to achieve 100 percent of project deliverables on time, every time.

## Project Priorities Change Constantly

As an individual or company, if you don't know where you're going, you will end up somewhere else.

This is also true for projects. The project team must know its priorities clearly. Normally, the project manager is responsible for setting up a priority list and keeping the team members informed. If project priorities change constantly, due to internal and external factors, the project team will have difficulty completing their tasks as required. No project manager likes to see this to happen, but in some companies priorities change daily.

The most common factors that cause constantly changing priorities are:

1. Changing market conditions. This happens mainly in long-duration projects. When the project duration is more than a year, there will usually be many changes in the marketplace. The project schedule may become very critical, which increases pressure on the team to work faster, or the project may become less important, resulting in resources being "robbed" for other more important projects. This is the main disadvantage of a long-duration project. The longer the duration, the more frequent are the changes and the more rework there will be.

2. Too many stakeholders or decision makers who have different interests in the project. For a big project where the project managers have to interface with many stakeholders, it is very difficult to have one common priority list to cover all the different interests. As such, a project manager may have no choice but to change the project priorities from time to time to cater to the special concerns of some stakeholders. In other cases, when there is more than one major decision maker in a project, it will be even more difficult to keep a common priority list for the team.

## Too Many Product Features

Before a new project is approved, it is normally justified with many new technological changes, enhanced with many new product features or functions that will impress customers. The more new product features and functions, the bigger the project team will be, and the longer the duration. However, as was previously stated, many of these new technological changes are yet to be tested and normally take time to prove. More importantly, their completion date is unpredictable. When a new project utilizes many new technological changes at the same time, it slows down.

To overcome this problem, we should apply a solution that was developed by the automobile industry a long time ago. This reliable solution is that they will make sure each new product will reuse at least 75 percent of existing technology and design. For the 20 to 25 percent new changes, only minor changes or proven "new technology" will be used in a new model. (Proven "new technology" refers to technology that is being used in another car). Just look at the new car models on the market and note that, very often, the only change is a face-lift, or application of a feature that is already being used in another model.

Reusing existing technology and design has another major advantage, which is that the project team will be smaller and the duration will be much shorter. This fits very well with the definition of right-on-time projects.

## Too Few Resources

No company has unlimited resources. Yet most companies undertake more projects than their resources allow for. When this happens, many people get assigned to several projects at once. (One company we know of has allocated people to projects at a 120 percent rate. That is, before a project starts, it is already decided that the project members will have to work overtime to meet the project schedule. This might be justifiable on a single project, but all of their projects are run this way!) Changing project scope to include more product functions and features affects other projects (and the resources needed to do this are normally pulled from lower-priority projects). Thus it is difficult to add the resources necessary to complete these new, unplanned tasks.

Where possible, you should allocate only full-time team members to a project. Often, when management tries to maximize its resource utilization, they assign staff to more than one project—these people are called "part-time" project members (e.g., 20 percent to one project, 30 percent to another project, and 50 percent to yet another). The net result of this approach is increased setup time as a person constantly shifts from one job to another. And setup time is waste.

To overcome this, it is clear that we must assign only full-time team members to a project. In addition, you should allocate only 80 to 85 percent of your resources to projects. Every system should have some reserve capacity to handle unexpected "turbulence."

## Poor Quality and Rework

Studies have found that about 30 percent of all project costs go to rework. This means one of every three people working on a project is spending all his or her time re-doing what two other people have done wrong. Two of the major reasons for rework are poor planning and ever-changing project scope. When project scope changes, the project team has no choice but to rework what is done to keep the project relevant, as was explained above. Poor planning—especially poor resource allocation—is another factor. A project member who is working on more than one project will quite often take shortcuts to save the time, which may increase errors and thus rework. Another cause of rework is unclear task requirements.

To overcome these problems, the project team must establish definitive quality expectations for the project and among the project team members. They must understand the quality requirements for completing a task and the next "customer's" expectations. These requirements and expectations must be discussed and documented up front. This minimizes disagreements and arguments later in the project life cycle. (This will be discussed in greater detail in Chapter 5.)

## Poor Planning

It has been said that if you fail to plan, you plan to fail. When a project is on a tight schedule or is perceived to be late, many project managers rush to start project work with no planning whatsoever. This is called a "ready-fire-aim" approach, which usually results in false starts, people going in the wrong direction, and much rework. There are two major problems with this approach:

1. Unilateral planning: In the rush to start up the project, and with all good intentions, the project manager plans the project for the group (sometimes by just telling the team what should be done, without any reason and/or references) and then turns it over to them to execute. The team is unlikely to commit to this plan and deliver work as required. For one thing, they often don't understand the plan, and the project manager's estimate of task durations is likely to be optimistic. In addition, the project manager is very likely to forget some major factor that will later intrude and cause significant delays.

2. The "ready-fire-aim" approach is adopted because of the belief that people could get the work done by the time they could prepare a proper plan. The truth is that the more important the deadline, the more important the plan. Only when you have forever is a plan unimportant. A simple way to understand this is to imagine trying to reach a destination in an unfamiliar location without benefit of a roadmap (a plan).

## Perfectionism

It is one thing to want to improve processes continuously. Perfectionism, however, is paralyzing, because by definition it can never be reached. The main reason for perfectionism is fear. Sometimes, you just do not know how the market will react to a new product. Will customers accept it? Because of fear of product rejection, the product definition grows until you have a "do-everything" product. This can only be avoided if marketing clearly defines product requirements in terms of "must-have," "wants," and "nice-to-have." In general, the product should only include the must-have features on the first release. The wants and nice-to-have features can be added to subsequent product releases.

## INSTALLING A PROCESS

When you have eliminated the causes of slowness in one project, your next step is to ensure that success for *every* project. While it is true that every project is unique, "Product development is one area where extra effort of process design is rewarded handsomely. It is one of the few nonrepetitive processes that warrants careful process design" (Reinertsen, 1997, p. 119). As such, you should establish a standard modular process that is specially tailored to your business and industry. This process should specify the unique requirements of your industry in the project life cycle (concept stage, definition stage, planning stage, execution stage, and closeout stage). The purpose of a standard modular process is to ensure that the project team has a template for planning, review, and other actions. Most importantly, it provides a common platform to share lessons learned from various projects.

The modular process is proposed by Donald G. Reinertsen, who writes: "The simplest approach to combining structure and flexibility is to build the development process out of modules. By altering the use and sequence of these modules we can produce millions of possible process configurations without losing control" (Reinertsen, 1997, p. 120). The modules are based on the particular design needs of the product being developed. These modules should have clear input and output requirements and spell out any special actions required of the cross-functional team.

For example, at the concept stage the standard modules include:

1.  Report on product market position.
2.  Benchmarking, competitive analysis.
3.  Business case (resource requirements, target price, quantity, and introduction schedule).
4.  Customer-needs analysis.
5.  New technology availability.

At the definition stage the standard modules include:

1.  Previous team lessons-learned report and recommended actions for future projects.
2.  Product final specification.
3.  Process and equipment specification.
4.  Final customer requirement specification.
5.  Updated business case (target price, quantity, and introduction schedule).
6.  Key suppliers/key component availability.
7.  Committed resources allocation plan.
8.  Quality plan and requirements.

At the planning stage the standard modules include:

1.  Project plan with WBS by week.
2.  Resource utilization plan.
3.  Process and equipment delivery schedule.
4.  Key components delivery schedule.
5.  Risk assessment.
6.  Contingency plan.
7.  Product introduction plan and timelines.

At the execution stage the standard modules include:

1.  Product prototype build.
2.  Engineering samples build.

3. Qualification samples build.
4. Pilot line setup, equipment setup.
5. Process verification and trial run.
6. Software verification; beta test module.
7. Design verification test module.
8. Design maturity test module.

At the project closeout stage the standard modules include:

1. Mass product run result.
2. Ongoing reliability test module.
3. Team lessons-learned workshop and results.
4. Final business case.

When you have established a modular process for product development and have clearly stated the requirements for each module, the project team will have more flexibility to plan and organize the project without losing control and quality. The content of each module will depend on the type of product being developed.

# 5

CHAPTER

# Resource Allocation:
# The Heart of Every Project

*The performance of a manager is measured
by how well that manager can organize a
large number of people and how effectively he
or she can get the highest performance from
each of the individuals and blend them into a
coordinated performance.*

— Akio Morita, Sony Chairman

"**P**eople are the most important asset in my company."

Every CEO or HR director will tell you this. But the people working in the company may tell you a different story. What managers *say* matters very little. What does matter is how *people assets* are utilized. This separates a great company from the rest. If project teams are to excel, resource allocation

*Assigning people to the right job at the right time is always a challenge.*

is a most important issue to address. There's a big difference between a project-oriented company and a manufacturing company. The skills required in new product development projects and those needed for production are totally different. In this chapter we focus on resource planning and allocation for new product development projects.

Many organizations have a HR policy that goes something like this. "We value people as our most important asset, and we treat them with respect, trust, and dignity. With mutual agreement, we will allocate the jobs that fit their individual personal profile so that they will reach their full potential."

However, assigning people with the right skill to the right job at the right time is always a challenge. Very few companies make a strong effort to achieve this goal. In fact, most companies just assign people to a project based on availability (not people's capability). Managers often say, "That's all we have; all my resources are used up." This problem can only be addressed by developing a proper resource planning system.

## RESOURCE PLANNING

Many managers confuse resource planning with recruitment. Resource planning has a much broader meaning than just hiring new people. Resource planning should be aligned with the company's vision and mission and its short- and long-term strategies. The question that should be asked is, "What type of people, with what kind of skills, do we need to achieve these strategic goals? How can we train and retrain our people in order to achieve these objectives?" These questions are answered by reference to the company's strategic intent.

### Strategic Resource Planning

This is long-term resource planning based on the company's strategy. For example, when a company wants to launch a new technology platform or enter into a new market, (such as moving from producing audio hi-fi systems to developing mobile phones), a unique kind of engineering staff will be required. It takes time and effort for a company to identify and recruit the required resources. Strategic resource planning, then, focuses on recruiting or developing existing resources for future needs.

Strategic resource planning is done to prepare and position the company for the future. It is also intended to make the difficult technological switchover easier. As stated above, identifying future staff requirements begins with understanding where the company wants to go. Once this is accomplished, a plan can be developed to train the existing workforce and recruit individuals with skills that are so specialized that training existing people is not possible.

Strategic resource planning takes inputs from the following areas:

1. Long-term strategies.
2. Long-term product roadmap.
3. Long-term technology roadmap.
4. Long-term supplier technology roadmap.

*Planning a project enables the project manager to control work and meet targets.*

The strategic resources plan should also divide the resource pool into two parts, one for new product projects, and one for technology building blocks. This is to ensure that the ratio of activities aimed directly at making money (product development projects) and activities aimed solely at preparing for the future (new technologies) are allocated properly and are within the company's means to control. Strategic resource planning is a continuous process that requires active participation from all management team members and should be led by the manager of innovation, R&D, or whatever group is charged with responsibility for product and technology development.

## Tactical Resource Planning

Tactical planning is an effort to make the best allocation of the *current* pool of resources. Tactical management of resources causes companies great headaches. There are almost always more projects than can be properly staffed.

The tactical resource plan reviews current resource conditions and makes necessary adjustments to support current project assignments. It is a summary of all projects, resource allocation, and status. Tactical resource allocation is the day-to-day operational aspect of managing projects.

Tactical planning requires inputs from the following areas:

1. Project priority list.
2. Product roadmap.
3. Technology building blocks.
4. Key components availability.
5. Inputs from various development councils and project managers.

Because tactical resource allocation is focused on short-term resource leveling, it is best handled by the functional departments. However, their role now is to support projects rather than consider their functional departments as having priority. And this means supporting the project management office (PMO) (if you have one), since this department or function is responsible for the monitoring and support of all of the projects within the company. The objective is to ensure that resources are allocated in the best interests of the company as a whole, not just to satisfy the egos of specific functional or project managers.

This will be a new way of managing projects for many companies. The main advantage of this change is to have the development manager focus on technical issues while project managers are focused on delivering the projects per plan.

## BASIC GUIDELINES FOR RESOURCE ALLOCATION

Here are some guidelines you should follow in order to make tactical resource planning work:

1.  Allocate only 80 to 85 percent of the overall resource
    availability to projects. We know that this is heresy
    in the minds of many managers, who have been in-
    doctrinated to think "lean and mean." The problem
    with the lean-and-mean approach to managing pro-
    jects is that every time some problem occurs, it
    throws everything into a tailspin. Manufacturing op-
    erations have long known that you do not want to
    load the facility beyond 85 percent capacity for any
    length of time, because when something does go
    wrong (a machine breaks down or raw materials are
    delayed), your entire operation is disrupted. If we
    lived in a steady-state universe, in which unforeseen
    problems never occurred, this rule would be unnec-
    essary; but so long as turbulence exists, we need
    some reserve capacity to handle it.

2.  Do not allocate resources for more than nine months.
    Any resource allocation longer than nine months is
    just a guess. In general, you can only make predic-
    tions about the next three to six months. Also, it
    makes more sense to focus on short-duration projects.
    The only exception to this rule is a project that is set
    up under pure-project conditions, in which all re-
    sources are assigned to that job on a full-time basis.
    For standard projects in which resources are shared
    across projects, this guideline is sound.

3.  If possible, allocate resources to only one project.
    Most managers believe that they can allocate re-
    sources to several projects on a shared basis, because
    they think that 30%+30%+40% is equal to 100%. It is
    not. That's because there is always time lost during
    the transition from one project to the next. This is
    called setup time in manufacturing, and we have
    known for a long time that it is wasteful. As a gen-
    eral rule, you should assign a person to a priority-
    one project, with a backup that he or she can work
    on in case of dead time on the first priority job.

4. Do not add more resources to a late project hoping that this will compensate for the delay: As "Brooks Law" says: "Adding people to an already late project may only make it later" (Brooks, 1975).

5. Each project member should do everything possible to make a project succeed, and this is not limited to his or her job scope alone. One project manager told Louis that he always has problems asking his team members to write meeting minutes. All members need the meeting minutes as a reminder of action assignments made during the meeting, or as a reference for critical project decisions. But everyone thinks that writing minutes is not his or her job.

The attitude that only certain activities fit into a person's job is detrimental to teamwork. To illustrate, in one instance a project member left some electrical components on a mechanical engineer's desk. The mechanical engineer was upset and complained to his functional boss that he was not a messenger and had no use for these electrical components. The complaint was later passed on to the project manager. It was then revealed that the mechanical engineer was supposed to check the components for dimensions and confirm if they would properly fit into the circuit board for which they were intended. It was indeed his job, but because of his belief that these were electrical components, and had nothing to do with mechanical design, he caused the company much wasted time.

## TECHNICAL/ DEVELOPMENT COUNCILS

Following is an experience related by Louis Wong:

Many years ago, when I was a newly minted quality engineer, I had great difficulties applying what I learned in school to my work. While some in-house training programs did help, I always found the training came too late. I found it was more helpful to discuss the issue or problem with my seniors, those who had more experience in quality. However, while these discussions were very helpful to me, many of them did not have time for such discussions of a specific subject. This problem persisted until I joined the quality council, where I could freely discuss the quality issues with the same professionals and learn from them.

This quality council was formed after we attended the quality college presented by Crosby Associates. The purpose of the quality council is to bring together the appropriate people to share quality management information on a regular basis. We found that the same approach can be applied to other development functions, such as software development, electrical development, and so on. This is very important when we allocate full-time engineers to a project, because many of them will not have all the experience needed to complete the task. A supporting structure must be available to help them resolve their technical issues. Development councils are formal structures that support project team members in resolving technical questions and form the backbone of the full-time project members' approach.

Development councils should be led by technical experts who are not allocated to projects and should be chaired by functional managers. For example, the software development council should consist of council members who are senior software development platform engineers, and the software development manager should chair it. The council should meet regularly and share information on technical developments. The project team can bring problems they encounter to the council for guidance. The council can advise the team on courses of action and may even assign an expert to help to solve a particular problem. However, the project team is always accountable for the results.

Some useful guidelines for a development council are:

1. The number of councils should be based on the company's needs. For example, you may need an engineering council, or you may need a process development council and an equipment development council if you find the engineering council is becoming too big. You may need a quality council, electrical development council, and so on. The critical

point is that development councils must have formal status.

2. Each council must have a clear mission and vision, and a clear area of responsibility and operation. The council must meet regularly, and all meetings should be recorded.

3. Development councils are also responsible for future technologies within their respective fields. The councils should also be responsible for the technology roadmap and how to build up the company's technical competence.

4. When the project team encounters specific technical problems that they cannot resolve, they may ask the technical council for advice. Before doing so, the project team must define the problem and specify the actions taken to address it and the results achieved. The council then looks into the problem and advises actions to be taken. If these actions do not resolve the problem, the council may assign a technical expert to assist. All actions must be documented and may be used for future technical papers or patent applications.

5. Each council should prepare design guidelines for project teams to follow. They are also responsible for publishing technical papers and preparing patent applications.

## Summary of Responsibilities

The major difference between old structures and the new, project-oriented organization structure is that the development, or technical, experts will always focus on technical issues as well as future technology development, while project and administrative work is left to the project manager to handle. This structure will clearly grow the technical competence of the organization in a faster, more organized manner than is possible when these roles are shared. Figure 5.1 shows a

**F I G U R E  5.1**

New Project-Oriented Organization Structure

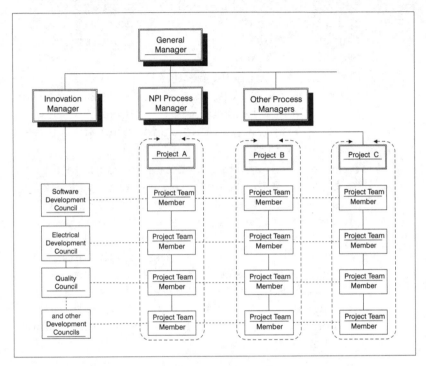

proposed new project-oriented structure (note: NPI = new product introduction).

## RESOURCE MONITORING

Resource utilization should be monitored closely but should not be overdone. Many companies require their project team members to record the time they spend on projects to the nearest fifteen minutes. If you are a lawyer or a consultant who charges your client an hourly rate, than this is fine, because most professionals bill in minimum increments of from one-tenth to one-quarter of an hour. However, this practice may create too much paperwork for the project team. Team members will not report the time during which they had coffee with their colleagues. Generally speaking, if you capture time to the nearest hour, your records will be good enough to determine development costs for new products.

One caution, however: People must record their time at the end of each day, whether they like it or not. If they wait until a week has passed to fill in their reports, they just guess at what they did, and this is not history, it is conjecture.

Another issue is that most engineers and other professionals are salaried. They are only paid for 40 hours a week, even though most of them work 50- and 60-hour weeks routinely. You must capture overtime worked on projects, even though it is unpaid, or on similar projects, when you use data from the previous project, your time estimates will be too low.

Keep in mind that this is not intended to punish people or to demonstrate that they are taking too long to do their work. Such an attitude only results in people falsifying their records. It must be recognized as a way of determining how long it really takes to do work so that the capacity of the resource pool will be certain. Without such data, your project "plans" are only guesses.

# 6
CHAPTER

# Project Monitoring
# and Control

*If you have no plan, you have no control!*

— Jim Lewis

**P**erhaps it goes without saying that the purpose of project management is to ensure that a project is completed on time, within budget and scope, and that the deliverable performs at the required level. Nevertheless, this is sometimes forgotten. Furthermore, the only reason for planning a project is to enable the project manager to control work so that these targets are met.

However, all the planning in the world will not ensure project control unless you have some way of measuring progress—that is, a way of knowing where you are. The definition of control is shown in the box. If you neglect any aspect of it, you can't have control. For example, if you know

> *Progress needs to be stated in measurable terms.*

that a deviation from plan exists but take no corrective action, then you are not controlling the job, you are simply monitoring it.

This does not mean that you get excited about every small deviation. There are tolerances in any control system. For example, the normal temperature control system in a room may vary about 6 degrees Fahrenheit, or about 3.5 degrees Celsius. Typically you can control construction projects to tolerances of about plus or minus 5 percent. For product development projects, this is likely to be around 15 to 20 percent. Trying to control any

> Control is exercised by comparing where you are to where you are supposed to be, and taking action to correct for any deviations from plan.

tighter than this means you are going to waste more time than you will gain benefits.

## MEASURING PROGRESS

In Chapter 3 I discussed the four constraints that apply to all projects: performance, cost, time, and scope (PCTS). To know the actual status of a project, you need to know the values of all four constraints. The easiest one to know is usually cost. This includes labor, materials, and capital equipment. In terms of *work progress*, only labor cost is tracked. Labor cost is the actual number of labor hours applied to the project multiplied by the labor rate paid to the people doing the work. Labor rate should always be expressed as *burdened rate*, not just the direct dollar-per-hour rate paid your employees. The burdened rate is the direct labor paid plus the overhead—what it costs the company for heat, water, utilities, rent, and employee benefits. This is the true cost per hour to do work. Unless you include overhead, your product development cost will be far too low.

> To know the real status of a project requires that you know about all four constraints—performance, cost, time, and scope.

Even though labor cost is usually easy to figure, many organizations have no system in place to track it accurately. Engineers, programmers, and scientists are often told to record only 40 hours per week for labor, even though they may actually work 60 hours on a project. This does not capture the true cost of the development effort, even though you do not pay for the 20 extra hours expended on the job.

A basic premise is that you do not want to plan a project so that overtime is required in order to meet original targets. If you do, and unexpected problems arise, as they always do, then you will not be able to use overtime to correct the problem. In addition, long periods of overtime have a severe effect on productivity. Studies have found that after about three weeks of overtime (at around 10 to 15 hours a week) productivity has declined to the normal 40-hour level, and errors have increased.

> Do not plan a project so that overtime is required to meet the original completion date.

This is bad enough, but what is often not measured is the indirect cost of absenteeism and turnover. When a professional person leaves because of job burnout, the cost to replace him or her is often $100,000 to $300,000! That's right. When you consider recruiting costs, loss of productivity while the replacement is learning the job, and agency fees paid, you find the cost to be extremely high. And even for skilled labor, the replacement cost is often in the tens of thousands of dollars. Turnover is expensive!

## A Pitfall

When I was a young engineer, I had to record my project time weekly. I filled out and turned in my report on Monday morning. At that time, I didn't know what I know now, which is the value of these reports. To me, it was just a bother. Now I understand that the reports are necessary to know if the project is under control.

> Working time should be recorded daily.

I also suffered from being unable to remember what I did a week prior to my report. We were supposed to record time at least to the nearest hour, but I had difficulty remembering if I was even at work on the previous Monday, much less what I worked on to the nearest hour, so I just put down what I believed I had done. I'm sure it was pure conjecture, but I didn't care. I had done my duty.

The only solution to this problem is to write down one's time at the end of the day. It takes about five minutes, which is not a big burden. However, I have had many knowledge workers complain about this becoming a burden—and I have concluded they are really afraid of accountability. They haven't worked productively, or they are taking longer to do something than they estimated and are afraid of the repercussions. I'm sorry, but accountability is something we must all accept in exchange for the salaries we receive.

I've also had them complain that they are professionals and shouldn't have to record time. My response is that if they worked as consultants, the client would expect them to record time, so that they wouldn't have to pay for time the consultant worked for another client.

No matter the reason, tracking time is essential for control purposes, and I suggest that it be to no more than one-hour increments. However, it also needs to be down to the task level, not just to the project. That is, every task in the schedule must be tracked individually. If people just charge time to the project, that is useless for control purposes.

## Tracking Performance, Time, and Scope

It can truly be hard to measure performance and scope in development projects. It is relatively easy for something like building a brick wall. Your plan says the wall should be 10 feet high, 50 feet long, and a certain thickness. You measure these dimensions; it turns out the wall is the correct length and thickness, but it is only 8 feet tall. This means that scope is only about 80 percent of what it should be. This also means the work is behind schedule. Although progress is not perfectly linear, the schedule performance is about 80 percent of target as well.

Performance is judged by inspection. The mortar between bricks looks good, the wall is nice and straight, and it
is properly vertical, as shown by a plumb bob. Of course,
there may be internal defects that inspection won't reveal,
but you simply can't be certain of everything, so you make
some assumptions.

Now try to apply this same measurement to knowledge
work! Where is the engineering design, exactly? Or the code
being written? Or the drawings being made? You simply cannot measure these like you can a brick wall. This is why I pre-
scribed the rule in Chapter 3 that knowledge work be broken
down into one- to three-week increments, with a "marker"
signifying completion. We do not pretend to know where the
work is during the week, only at the end of the week. It
should be complete. Either it is or it isn't. This is the best we
can do. Our control will be more granular than is the case
with other systems, but it will be functional to an acceptable
tolerance.

## The Flaw in Most Tracking Systems

It may be that 80 percent of all project tracking is done using
Microsoft Project® (or some similar scheduling software).
Schedule status is shown by running a small bar inside the
normal bars in the Gantt chart, as shown in Figure 6.1.

If you examine this schedule carefully, you will note
that the weekends are shown as shaded vertical areas, and
the schedule bars simply cross over them. Because they are
shaded, we know that no work is scheduled on weekends. If
it were, weekend days would not be shaded.

According to this schedule, task C is complete, task A is
one day behind schedule, task E is right on target, and task D
is one day ahead. Overall, the project seems in pretty good
condition. (Now, it is important to remember that this information is provided by the people doing the work.)

If you were the project manager, you would no doubt
feel pretty secure. No major problems are evident with the

# F I G U R E   6.1

## A Progress Report Using a Gantt Chart

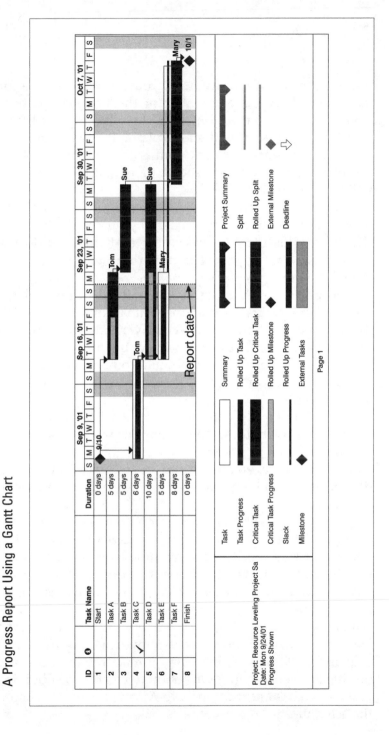

project. However, shortly after you receive status information from everyone, a member of the team drops by your desk and casually mentions that she felt sorry for Mary last week. You ask why, and she explains that Mary had a very difficult time with her work. Rather than taking the 40 hours she had planned to work, she actually had to work nearly 80 hours to get the job done.

This is a surprise to you, but then, Mary is a salaried worker so there has been no cost to your project budget, and she is on schedule. So, you agree that this is unfortunate, but it is now in the past. The only thing to do is get on with the job.

Some of you reading this may not have fully realized the implication of Mary's situation. If she estimated she could do the work in 40 hours and actually needed 80 hours, then something is potentially very wrong. If her estimate last week was off by 100 percent, why should you believe her future estimates will be correct? They may be, but you shouldn't take this for granted.

The thing to do is to ask Mary what is going on. There are several possibilities. One is that this was a fluke and Mary is confident that future work will not give her the same difficulty. In this case, you tell her to let you know if this assumption turns out to be wrong, so you can help her in whatever way you can.

Another possibility, however, is that Mary has come up against a "moment of truth." She realizes that she is in over her head. This work is taking much longer than she estimated, and there is no reason to believe this is going to change. Now you have to make some decisions. You may have to replace Mary with someone who can do the work as scheduled. Or, if nobody is available to do this, you may have to reschedule the work to show it taking twice as long as planned. This, of course, may impact the project end date, but it may be necessary. Or you may be able to subdivide the work so that someone can help Mary and thereby maintain the schedule.

One thing is certain—if Mary continues to work 80 hours a week for an extended period, you will come into the work area one day and find her collapsed on the floor. Furthermore, the quality and quantity of her work will get worse and worse.

> Reporting schedule progress alone does not reveal problems with the effort being expended on a project.

The key point here is that reporting schedule progress alone does not provide vital information about the *work effort* being expended to stay on schedule, and when that level of effort is excessive, it indicates a problem that you need to address. For this reason, as I said earlier, you need to measure *both* time and cost (as well as performance and scope).

One common way to do this is a method called earned-value analysis. I have found that most organizations struggle with this approach, so I recommend that you initially just track schedule and cost in simplified form. Then, as your organization becomes more adept at managing projects, you can migrate to earned-value tracking. For in-depth material on using the earned-value approach, see my book, *Project Planning, Scheduling, and Control*.

## REPORTING PROGRESS

One widespread method of showing progress is the "stoplight" approach. Beside each task being tracked are one or two cells that are colored red, yellow, or green to indicate status. Green, of course, means the task is on schedule and budget. Yellow suggests concern about status, and red means that there is a definite problem. If you use two cells, the first one indicates status last week and the second status for the current week (or reporting period, if different than a week).

These simplified reports should always be backed up by hard data, so that any problem areas can be examined to determine their threat.

## SOME SUGGESTIONS AND CAUTIONS

I have sat through many status meetings, and have observed some common flaws that should be avoided.

First, any problems that exist in a project should be dealt with outside the status meeting. Trying to solve problems during the status meeting bogs everything down and wastes the time of all attendees who are not directly involved in that aspect of the job. The

> Don't try to solve project problems in a status review meeting—move these to a special meeting.

problem should be dealt with in a special meeting that is scheduled after the status meeting ends.

Also, there should be no bloodletting in the review meeting. Even if people are "guilty" of actual misconduct, they should be confronted in private, not in public. Chastising people in front of others only leads to hard feelings, decreased morale, and a pervasive decline in incentive. Those members of the

> Never chastise someone in a meeting—never!

group who are not chastised know that it may be their turn next week, and everyone becomes overly cautious and risk-averse. This can be especially bad in an innovation project, because it often leads to "ho-hum" products.

Consider that what you really want to do about problems in projects is solve them. Your objective is not to beat up on people who have them. In addition, it is clear that if you have no problems, it may mean that everyone is playing it too safe.

My book *Working Together* (Lewis, 2001) describes principles for managing projects that were originally developed by Alan Mulally, who is now president and CEO of Boeing

Commercial Airplanes. Several of these principles are important to follow in monitoring projects.

## Clear Performance Goals

If every member of a project team is not clear about his or her performance goals, and how these will be measured, you have a prescription for disaster. In establishing goals, you should ask two questions:

What is the desired outcome?

How will we know it has been achieved?

The way in which the second question is asked allows for those situations in which no tangible deliverable is produced. Knowing the outcome has been achieved may only be possible qualitatively, rather than quantitatively.

## The Data Sets Us Free

Status reports that conclude "I think it's okay" or perhaps "It's fine" leave much to be desired. As I said, it is fine to use a stoplight report, but it should be backed up by data that validates the stoplight information. It is amazing how often problems are described in vague terms. "There's too much thinner in the paint." How much is too much? Is it just a small amount or a large amount? By providing a measurement, people can tell how serious the problem actually is.

"We're working too much overtime." This is a judgment. Is the actual level two hours a week? Ten hours? Twenty hours? Unless we know the actual number, we have no idea if the problem is serious or not.

## You Can't Manage a Secret

When people are afraid of being chastised for having a problem, they may hide it from everyone. Doing so prevents any action being taken to solve the problem. This may not be too serious if the problem affects only one group, but in projects this is never true for very long because all components of a project are interdependent. A problem in one area will eventually affect all of the others.

Dr. Edwards Deming (Deming, 1986) advocated encouraging employees to bring problems to everyone's attention so that those problems could be addressed. It is definitely a good practice to follow.

## Whining Is Okay—Occasionally

It is common for managers to dislike emotion in the workplace, but it is a fact that human beings are emotional creatures, and the best policy is to allow people to "vent" occasionally. Let them express their fears, concerns, or even anger, so long as it does not get out of hand. To require them to suppress their feelings just means that they will come out somewhere else, and usually in a destructive form.

## Propose a Plan, Find a Way

Still, we are all paid by organizations to solve problems, not just whine about them, so after we have vented, we are all expected to propose a solution. As I said earlier, this should be done in a special meeting rather than in the status meeting, but it should be done.

Only if a person has tried to solve a problem and has been unsuccessful should he or she ask for help. If the individual is unsure of his or her authority to implement certain courses of action, then someone in authority can be consulted, but this is not the same as dumping problems onto managers to solve.

## Listen to and Help One Another

The word "team" is sometimes forgotten in projects. Unless it is a one-person project, there will be others involved, and the climate should be one of cooperation and collaboration. In addition, you can't help someone unless you listen carefully to what they are saying. This practice promotes better teamwork and communication in any project team.

## IN SUMMARY

It is important to remember that the purpose of monitoring progress in a project is to ensure that it is completed on time, on budget, and at the correct scope and performance levels. This is another way of saying you are trying to exercise control. However, the word "control" often denotes the idea of controlling *people*, and this is not what you are trying to do! Rather, you are trying to *control the project work, not the people*. In fact, the only way you will ever exercise control as a manager is if every member of your team has control of his or her own work.

This cannot be achieved through micromanaging, either. You must establish conditions whereby every individual is able to exercise self-control, and you intervene only when that individual demonstrates that he or she can't quite exert the control necessary to keep work on track. In the same way that you need an overall project plan to have control, every individual must be planning his or her own work at a sufficient level of detail to maintain control. You don't need to consolidate these plans into the project master plan—to do so would result in a huge, unwieldy plan. But you do need to see to it that the individual plans are being made.

Consider this. If any individual in your team goes out of control, she will eventually sink your entire project. If she uses up all of the float, she winds up on the critical path, and from that point on, every additional minute she slips pushes out the project end date by that same amount.

Finally, progress needs to be stated in measurable terms. Having people say, "We're on track" is nearly useless. This is the one flaw in stoplight reporting. It allows people to "happy talk" themselves and others. Engineers are notorious in thinking they will solve technical problems in a flash, when in fact they have no idea how long it will actually take. Unless you impose a healthy dose of skepticism on the team, it is easy for everyone to fall into this trap.

This does not mean that you should become a tyrant and go around beating on everyone to determine their progress. It does mean that you take an active interest in progress, and let everyone know that your concern is solving problems, not attacking the staff.

# 7

# Risk Management

*If you hit every time, your target is either too big or too near.*

— Tom Hirshfield, Physicist

*If you want to maintain peace, be prepared for war.*

— Sun Tzu, *The Art of War*

*There is a higher probability that things will accidentally go wrong than that they will accidentally go right.*

— Murphy's Law

**W**hat is risk?

The answer is that risk is simply something that may happen unexpectedly.

*Once potential risks have been identified, the team should assess the impact on the project.*

There are two types of risk—positive and negative. Positive risk is often called *opportunity*, and as our friend Murphy has said, is not as likely as negative risk. Furthermore, most people are not concerned about positive risks, so in dealing with risk management, we will focus only on negative risk—those things that can unexpectedly go wrong.

Actually, most people don't even consider positive risk, so when we refer to risk, we are referring to negative events. Risk then has the following characteristics: (1) it may or may not happen (uncertainty or probability); (2) you can estimate this probability; (3) if it happens, it will result in some negative impact on the project (it could be cost, schedule, quality, or reputation); and (4) we may or may not be able to do something to reduce the impact (mitigation).

Risk management is therefore an informed, systematic approach to minimize the company's risk exposure. One very important concept is that "Risk management does not deal with the future decisions, but with the future consequences of present decisions" (Firth, 1999). In fact, it has been said that everything we do in project management is actually aimed at managing risk.

It is important that risk management not be so risk averse that no risks are taken, because without risk there is no innovation or entrepreneurship. It is senior management's role to decide how much risk the company will accept in pursuit of business objectives. The project team's job is to assess all project risks and take proactive steps to deal with them within the boundaries established by management.

## PROACTIVE RISK MANAGEMENT

The *reactive* approach to risk is to wait until something goes wrong and then decide what to do about it. Unfortunately, under such conditions, it is often very difficult to recover from the event. The *proactive* risk management process is to identify, assess, quantify, and manage risk (through planning) within a project in a timely and active manner so as to maximize the chances for the project's success. Proactive risk management should be done at the very outset of the project and be reviewed and updated throughout the project. Risk assessment should be done for each project phase. The findings, risk prevention actions, and contingency planning should be presented to management at each management review meeting. Management should focus on the following key distinct activities:

1. *Risk management planning.* This should be done at the beginning of the project, at the project definition and planning stages. The main objective is to define the

*approach* that will be used to examine all potential
risks that are associated with the project. This is critical. All potential risks should be properly reviewed,
analyzed, quantified, and communicated to the project team, the project sponsor, and the sponsor organization based on their importance and potential
impact on the organization. Risk management planning should specify responsibilities and requirements, and outline tools and techniques that will be
employed.

A risk management plan is a summary of all the
action plans used to identify, assess, quantify, and
prioritize project risks, in order to determine contingency plans, or to identify the triggering points for
actions and subsequent management review. This
plan should be updated prior to every management
review meeting. Any actions taken and decisions
made should be documented and reviewed again at
the next management review meeting.

2. *Risk identification.* Risk identification is the first step in
the risk management process. The project team members determine what kind of risks may impact the
project and define the characteristics of each of them.
The simplest way to identify risks (since we are considering only negative risks) is to ask, "What might
go wrong?" Like risk management planning, risk
identification should be done at the beginning of the
project (i.e., project definition and planning stages).
This is important because if the team identifies a major risk at this stage, it may better to cancel the project
or alter the project scope to reduce that risk.

For example, suppose the customer expects that
a new product will be available within nine months,
but the project employs a new technology that is
still being developed and will not be released for
eight months. Like any new technology, there is a
very high risk that it will be delayed. Thus it is es-

sential for the project team to identify this as a high risk and discuss this issue with the customer. The outcome may be that the customer is willing to accept a delay in delivering the new product, or has a contingency plan ready. The contingency plan may not be the best solution—it may be either more costly or have fewer features than the new technology—but it will be an acceptable alternative if the cutting-edge technology can't be delivered on time.

3. *Risk assessment.* Once potential risks have been identified, the team should assess the impact on the project should they occur. This would include such factors as commercial risks (market conditions, competitor response, etc.), technical risks (new key component development, new technologies), and project risks (budget, time, resources, and scope). These include both qualitative risk analysis and quantitative risk analysis. The main objective is to assess and quantify the exposure to the project and sponsor organization. This risk assessment should be repeated throughout the project at different stages (i.e., execution and closeout). Many good analytical tools are available for assessing risks, but remember, they are just tools. The project team's judgment will be critical if the assessment is to be meaningful.

   There are also existing techniques for thinking through a problem or situation that do not involve statistical methods. Often the risks identified do not lend themselves to hard data.

   Furthermore, analytical techniques can produce a false sense of precise measurement, even when estimates of probability and exposure are being made. These statistical methods generally require a large population of data to be valid. What is most important is that the team must constantly reassess the potential risks and make new judgments about them.

Following are some of the most commonly used analytical tools used for risk assessment.

## Tools for Risk Assessment

**Failure mode and effect analysis (FMEA):** This is a quantitative method in which design engineers identify the possible modes of failure for various components and production processes (which we also call process FMEA). Based on past data from similar components and processes, the team will then identify the probability and severity of the failure mode and calculate a risk priority number (RPN). Tables are used to do this, but as a simple example, say that a low probability of occurrence gets a value of 1, a moderate probability of occurrence a value of 5, and a high probability a 9. For severity, if the impact will be negligible, you assign an index of 1; for moderate impact a value of 5; and for severe impact, a value of 9. In addition, you ask whether the failure can be detected easily. If not, an index of 9 may be used, if the answer is moderate a 5 is assigned, and if it is easy to detect, you use a value of 1.

So assume that you have two possible failure modes. Notice in the following table that the RPN is the same for each possible failure, but in one case the severity is 9 and in the other the severity is 1. Clearly, the failure mode with the highest severity would be a "show stopper," while the other would not (Table 7.1).

Using the data generated in this analysis, engineers then decide what to do about the various failure modes.

This technique can be used to analyze any kind of risk, including non-engineering risk. In such a case, you may want to drop detection, and use just probability and severity as your "measures." This yields what might be called simply a risk index (RI). Naturally the numbers have no absolute or exact meaning. They are subjective in nature. Nevertheless, they give you a tool by which to make important decisions about how various risks should be handled. In general, when

**T A B L E  7.1**

Comparison of Two Different Failure Modes

| Mode | Probability | Severity | Detection | RPN |
|------|-------------|----------|-----------|-----|
| 1 | 1 | 9 | 5 | 45 |
| 2 | 9 | 1 | 5 | 45 |

a failure mode has a high severity, it is best to try to avoid the outcome entirely.

Simulations: This is also a quantitative method that involves manipulating a set of variables through all likely combinations to develop a most likely result. The most common application in project management is to test the project schedule duration and its dependencies, although it can be used on cost estimates as well. The most frequently used simulation method, the Monte Carlo technique, varies task duration over some predetermined range of values, and calculates the critical path for each random combination. These calculations may be made a thousand times to generate a distribution of critical-path durations. This allows assessment of the probability that the project will be completed by a certain time. The validity, of course, is only as good as one's ability to model likely variations. A software program called @RISK works with Microsoft Project to do such simulations.

This technique can also be used to simulate component usage for different application conditions such as temperature, vibration, component tolerances, or other factors, which allows designers to identify the boundary conditions of a component design. To ensure a valid result, Monte Carlo and other simulation methods require the use of sophisticated computer software and user-defined conditions. Putting aside the computer resources availability and cost issues, the most difficult part is for the users to specify all the possible test conditions, schedules, and their dependencies. Thus simulation methods are generally used only in very complicated or important projects.

Early tests (chicken tests): This quantitative method requires the team to conduct special tests to evaluate some of the key components or subprojects before proceeding to the next step. This is a reality test of extreme conditions. The chicken test is named after the approach by jet engine designers in which bodies of dead chickens are hurled at the intake of a jet engine to ensure that it will survive a hit from a bird during flight. Like the chicken test for the jet engine, the project team must evaluate certain project risks as early as possible to determine if their impact on the project might be catastrophic.

Risk implication matrix (RIM): Another quantitative method, very similar to FMEA, that requires the team to quantify risks using the values shown in Table 7.2.

Risk description: Outlines the risk that is being evaluated.

Severity: Describes the impact on the project or company should the risk occur. For example, if the problem is a safety issue, it will be rated as 5 (highest).

Probability: The chance that the risk will happen. The highest score is unknown= 5.

Exposure: The cost to fix the problem or the loss that will result to the company.

Risk Index: The product of severity, probability, and exposure. This risk index can be used as a reference for prioritizing the project risks.

Contingency plan: The alternative action that will be followed to avoid or to prevent the risk, or, if this is not possible, the mitigation steps to be taken if the risk actually occurs.

**T A B L E  7.2**

Comparison of Two Different Failure Modes

## Risk Implication Matrix (RIM)

| S/N | Risk Description | Severity (Safety=5, Major problem=4, Med problem=3, Minor problem=2, No problem=1), | Probability (Unkown=5, H=4, M=3, L=2, unlikely=1) | Exposure (Potential Cost) | Risk Index (S × P × E) | Contingency (Alternative action plan) | Triggering Point (When) |
|---|---|---|---|---|---|---|---|
| | | | | | | | |
| | | | | | | | |
| | | | | | | | |
| | | | | | | | |
| | | | | | | | |
| | | | | | | | |
| | | | | | | | |
| | | | | | | | |
| | | | | | | | |

Triggering point: This is the date and time that the project team must act to implement the contingency plan.

The risk implication matrix is useful for prioritizing risks and communicating them to management for support and endorsement.

Delphi technique: This qualitative method requires several experts in specific fields to state what they see as the top 5 to 10 project scope requirements. Based on these top requirements, each expert lists the major risks and indicates their impacts on the project. The organizer of this analysis then consolidates all the experts' answers into a complete list of potential risks. This method depends on the individual expert's personal experiences and judgments, and sometimes there may be conflicting views that make the assessment very difficult. These differences, however, form the basis for discussing the issues and arriving at an approach that the experts can support.

Strengths-weaknesses-opportunities-threats (SWOT): T h i s qualitative method provides an organized way of assessing the ability of the project team to execute the job successfully. To conduct a SWOT analysis, the team answers the following questions:

1. What strengths do we have, and how can we take advantage of them?
2. What weaknesses do we have, and how can we minimize the impact they will have on the project?
3. What opportunities are there, and how can we capitalize on them?
4. What threats to the project exist? What can we do to eliminate or minimize them?

(**Note:** You can download a form for conducting a SWOT analysis from my web site: www.lewisinstitute.com.)

Using the SWOT analysis, the team can develop an action plan to address the weaknesses and threats and formulate ways to take advantage of strengths and opportunities.

Force-field analysis: This is also a qualitative method, in which the project team concentrates on the potential actions of people. It essentially addresses the political environment for the project. Two questions are asked. The first is, What social or political forces will help us succeed? The second is, What social or political forces may cause us difficulty? Once these are identified, the idea is to estimate the strength of each force, and then compare the positive forces with the negatives. If the sum of the positive forces does not exceed the strength of the negatives, your project is headed for failure. This is a difficult exercise to quantify and therefore is best done by attempting to find ways to accommodate or neutralize the resistance. Other areas to concentrate on when performing a force-field analysis could include feelings or perceptions of other nonrelated groups that could have a negative impact on the project.

## Risk Response Control Plan

Once risks have been identified and quantified, it is time to develop a plan on how to handle the risks that have been selected for action (there is no need to take action for risks that are unlikely to have any impact on the project). Based on the risk assessments, the team should prioritize them according to their severity, probability, and exposure and should recommend actions to handle these risks. These actions may include:

Avoidance: You can avoid the risk. This often means finding the root cause of the risk and eliminating it. For example, suppose there is a risk of hostile community relationships due to an industrial installation near a neighborhood. This actually happened in a mill town. The company avoided the problem by offering to purchase the residents' houses for twice the appraised value. Those homeowners who had objected eventually accepted the offer and moved.

Transference: It may be possible to transfer the consequence of a risk to another organization. Transference is widely used, especially for large projects that cost millions of dollars. There are two ways in which this can be done. One is to contract the work to another group. The second is to purchase insurance to cover the risk. Either way, the risk exposure has been transferred to someone else. In the case of insurance, the downside is that the organization is required to pay a risk premium to the insurance company. In the case of contracting out the work, you lose direct control over it.

Mitigation: You can also reduce the risk by reducing its probability and/or the impact on the project. For example, the new product is more likely to be completed on time if the scope of the project is reduced; more frequent tests are conducted to ensure problems are detected early; or a more stable and proven production process is implemented. Other examples are the seat belts and airbags in your car. Their objective is to reduce the chances of the risk occurring or its impact. Tudor Rickards has suggested that seat belts and airbags actually increase the probability of an accident because people have a false sense of security should they have an accident. He has (not entirely jokingly) suggested that a better approach may be to place spikes across the dashboard so that drivers are sure they will be injured should they hit something. Doing so would cause them to be more careful (Rickards, 1975).

Acceptance: It is a sometimes-viable strategy to simply accept a risk if it occurs. This approach should be coupled with a "what-if" scenario and a triggering action if the risk occurs. For example, in the digital phone market, since the time-to-market is the most critical factor, the manufacturer may be willing to offer "patches" or quick fixes online for minor firmware bugs or "un-user-friendly" features found in the product, rather than delay the new product launch.

## Risk Handling and Tracking

The last step in proactive risk management is to continue to assess the identified risks, track the status (or changes), and update the response actions. It is also important to continue to identify new risks in the project. No project is static—every project will change over time. This is a continuous process that will only be completed when the project is completed or terminated.

## RISK MANAGEMENT REVIEW

If you do not actively attack and prevent risks in advance, they will catch up with you one day. Management should therefore enforce proper risk management in a project. While the project team should handle the detailed actions, such as risk management planning, risk identification and assessment, and risk response planning (as discussed above), the team must communicate these findings and actions to management for endorsement. This is because these decisions will have great implications not only for the project alone, but also for the organization, sponsor(s), and stakeholders. Therefore, management must fully understand the implications of these project risk decisions for the organization as a whole.

All risks must be clearly identified and quantified, and response actions provided. A proper format is therefore necessary for consistency and easy management review. The risk implication matrix (RIM) is a good tool for the project team to use to monitor and track the risk action plan. In preparing for the management review, the team should summarize the risks in a simple and easy-to-understand format for management to endorse. Many companies have applied a tool called the maturity grid for management review and making decisions. The maturity grid is used to judge whether the risks and their action plans are acceptable before the team continues with the project. As we have seen in Chapter 1, the biggest investment for a new product development project is made at the time when the new product is ready for production. To minimize cash flow and cost problems, it is better to terminate a doomed project as early as possible. Senior managers make this decision, so they need solid information on risks as early in the project as possible. The maturity grid is also used to communicate project readiness.

## RISK ASSESSMENT AT PROJECT CONCEPT PHASE

At the project concept phase, management should review project risks and decide if the project should be implemented. So that management can make this determination, the project team should assess project feasibility in all areas– including market risk, project scope, and timing risk, as well as re- source and technology risks. The first risk management meet- ing should include participants and representatives from marketing and sales, product quality, manufacturing, devel- opment, engineering, and the core project team members. The team should identify potential risks in their respective areas and, together as a team, assess the risks and produce a response plan. The risks should be prioritized, and risk re- sponse actions defined, in the risk implication matrix. The team should then translate the risks into the project maturity grid using the following criteria.

### Project Risk Severity

Market and customer risk (M) (market stop): The project is not feasible to implement due to a lack of market or no ma- jor customers. This is a showstopper for the project. The team is required to prepare a response action plan and a contingency plan.

Project timing risk (T) (time stop): The project cannot be com- pleted within the time frame specified. This is also a show- stopper for the project, and the team is required to prepare a response action plan and contingency plan.

Project resources risk (R) (resources stop): The project team does not have all the necessary resources to implement this project. This includes human resources (project team members) and funding. This is a showstopper for the project, and management is required to allocate the necessary resources or place the project in jeopardy. The project team is required to prepare a proposal to manage the situation.

**Project scope risk (S) (scope stop):** The project scope, product functions, and features are not feasible to execute because new technology is not yet ready or staff lacks the know-how to operate it. This is another showstopper. The team is required to prepare a response action plan and contingency plan.

**Acceptable risk (D) (accepted risk):** The project team has identified the potential risks but found they are not critical or are acceptable. These risks do not affect project implementation but do require continued monitoring and assessing to see if their attributes change during project implementation.

## Evolution Factors

**Level 5:** Risks are identified but not yet evaluated.

**Level 4:** Risks are identified and assessed but there is no response and action plan to address the risk. Contingency plan is not available.

**Level 3:** Risks are identified and assessed, a response and an action plan are prepared, and a contingency plan is available. However, the effectiveness of these plans has not been assessed or agreed upon within the project team and among the project stakeholders.

**Level 2:** The response action plan and contingency plan have been reviewed and accepted. This plan is not yet included in the overall project plan for execution.

**Level 1:** The risk response action plan is part of the overall project plan for monitoring and tracking.

Based on the above classification and the documented risks in the RIM, the team can now summarize the risks into the project maturity grid, as shown in Figure 7.1. This will provide management with a clear idea of the risks associated in this project. For example, if there is a risk of delaying the project due to unavailability of new technology, but the team has not assessed how long this new technology may be delayed, or has failed to assess its impact on the project, then this would be a T-5 Risk scenario. "1" (as indicated, 1 risk) will be placed in the T-5 square. If you have another

**F I G U R E  7.1**

Project Maturity Grid—For Project at Conceptual, Definition, and Planning Phase

|  |  | Market & customer risk | Project timing risk | Project resources risk | Project scope risk | Acceptable risks |
|---|---|---|---|---|---|---|
|  |  | **M** | **T** | **R** | **S** | **D** |
| Risk is not evaluated | **5** |  |  |  |  |  |
| Risk response plan is not finalized | **4** |  |  |  |  |  |
| Risk response plan is not proven | **3** |  |  |  |  |  |
| Risk response plan agreed | **2** |  |  |  |  |  |
| Risk response plan is part of the project plan | **1** |  |  |  |  |  |

risk related to another problem that may cause another delay, then the number will be increased accordingly. The shaded zone represents major risks for which management attention is required.

## RISK ASSESSMENT AT THE PROJECT DEFINITION PHASE

At the project definition phase, management is to review with the project team the final definition, scope, and specifications for the project. This is a critical stage, as it will finalize project requirements before the team can proceed with planning. This is also the last opportunity for the team to agree with the project sponsor and project beneficiaries on project deliverables. The project team must state clearly the deliverables of the project in a project charter that summarizes all project details, in agreement with the project sponsor. The risk assessment should also cover the unfinished items from the previous risk assessment at the project concept phase. However, risk assessment at this stage should focus primarily on risks related to project definition.

### Project Risk Severity

The same factors are examined in this phase that were examined at concept phase—market feasibility, schedule, resources, scope, and so on.

### The Evolution Factors

The evolution factors are also the same as those examined in the concept phase.

Once again, these factors are entered into the risk implication matrix. Management will decide whether to proceed with the project, cancel it, or modify requirements so it can continue.

## RISK ASSESSMENT AT THE PROJECT PLANNING PHASE

At the project planning phase, management is to review project risk and decide if the project plan covers the whole project, including adequate risk response and action. Management should also determine if there are any changes in market conditions that may affect the project. The same procedure is applied to this phase that was used in previous phases to examine project risk severity, evolution factors, and the risk implication matrix, again to determine the disposition of the project. This procedure is often referred to as a stage-gate process, which enables management to decide whether a project should continue or be terminated at each major step.

## RISK ASSESSMENT AT THE PROJECT IMPLEMENTATION PHASE

For new product development projects, the focus of risk assessment at this phase will be on the development of the product and customer acceptance. In general, additional risks are often found during the design verification test (DVT) and design maturity test (DMT). The team should use the RIM to document, monitor, and track all these risks, as was done at previous phases. The product maturity grid is the most effective tool to report risks to management (see Figure 7.2).

Following are a few guidelines specific to this phase that should be considered.

### Product Risk Severity

Safety or environmental risk (S): During the DVT and DMT, a product found to have safety risk or environmental risk must be corrected immediately. This is a showstopper for the project. The team is required to prepare a response action plan and a contingency plan.

**Not sellable or not producible (A):** Based on the DVT and DMT tests, there are major defects that cause this product to be unsaleable or unproducible. This is a showstopper for the project. The team is required to prepare a response action plan and a contingency plan.

**Not acceptable by major customers or produce with major difficulties (B):** The problem detected will not be accepted by major customers and/or production will have difficulties producing the product. This is a showstopper. The team is required to prepare a response action plan and contingency plan.

**Can be sold or produced with minor difficulties (C):** The problem detected will be accepted by most customers but will not be improved at the mass production stage; or the problem may cause minor production problems. This is a not showstopper. The team is required to prepare a response action plan to resolve this problem.

**Risks are identified and accepted (D):** The project team has identified potential risks but found they are noncritical or are acceptable. These risks do not affect the implementation of the project but require continued monitoring and assessment to determine if their attributes change during project implementation.

## Evolution Factors

**Level 5:** The root cause of the problem is unknown. This is rated as the highest risk.

**Level 4:** Corrective action is not yet finalized. This is rated as second highest risk. The team must come up with corrective action as soon as possible.

**Level 3:** The corrective action has been determined but not yet verified or proven.

**F I G U R E  7.2**

Product Maturity Grid—For New Product Development Project
at Implementation Phase

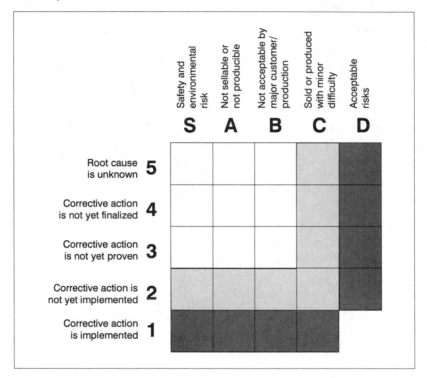

**Level 2:** The corrective action is verified to be effective but is not yet implemented.

**Level 1:** The corrective action is both implemented and effective.

The project and product maturity grids are very useful tools for management. They provide a clear, concise overview of project risks and response and action plans at different project phases. Management uses them to understand individual project risk issues and their impacts on the organization before reaching final project decisions.

Many companies have also adopted the traffic light system to highlight critical problems. Any problem that falls into the "red zone" (up to B-3) is considered a "red alert" and requires special management attention.

# 8

## CHAPTER

# Project Quality Management

*Quality management is a systematic way of guaranteeing that organized activities happen the way they are planned. . . . Doing things right the first time adds nothing to the costs, doing things wrong is what costs money.*

—Philip Crosby

**W**hat is project quality management? And why does it matter?

First, let's state why it matters. Studies continue to find that one reason for poor project performance is rework, largely due to inadequate planning. Crosby's quote above says it all: doing things right the first time does not add to the cost of work. It is rework that is wasteful, and the studies

*Rework is largely due to inadequate planning. Project quality cannot be overlooked.*

consistently find that it accounts for about 30 percent of project costs. For that reason, project quality management is one of the most important, yet overlooked, activities that you should consider in accelerating your projects.

Clearly, if you can reduce or eliminate rework, you can do your jobs faster and cheaper at the same time. This means that you reach breakeven faster with new products, giving you some protection from competitors who might follow you very quickly with their own products. Furthermore, you reduce the probability that you may have to cancel a product development project because the product will never yield the required return on investment (because you have reduced the investment). Building in steps that reduce rework through improved quality is a no-brainer!

## SIMULTANEOUS PRODUCT AND PROCESS DEVELOPMENT

Two major factors affect final product quality. One is design; the other is the manufacturing process. Both must be carried out properly. If you design a perfect product and produce it using a flawed process, the final product will not conform to its requirements. Likewise, the best manufacturing process cannot produce a perfect product from a flawed design. For that reason, the best way to accelerate a product development project is to design the product and the manufacturing processes simultaneously. This approach will be described in subsequent sections of this chapter.

## PROJECT QUALITY MANAGEMENT DEFINED

*The Guide to the Project Management Body of Knowledge* (*PMBOK® Guide*) suggests that project quality management includes the processes required to ensure that the project will satisfy the needs for which it was undertaken (*PMBOK* 2002, p. 95). It covers three major processes:

1. **Quality planning:** Planning how to assess and ensure that the project will meet the project specifications and related quality standards.

2. **Quality assurance:** Conducting tests and evaluations to assess whether the project meets quality requirements and standards.

3. **Quality control:** Monitoring project progress against the pre-established plan and ensuring that proper corrective actions are taken if project work fails to meet quality requirements.

This generic project quality management system is suitable for all different types of projects.

For new product development projects, while we will also follow these main processes, we focus more on the specific aspect of the new product development project quality management systems (NPD-PQMS) that cover the following areas:

1. **Design quality:** This is ensured by planning, assessing, and verifying at the beginning of the project whether the design of the new product conforms to all design rules and specifications. This includes both software and hardware designs.

2. **Product quality/product design validation:** Achieved through the planning, assessment, and

verification of whether the final product conforms to the product specifications. This includes all the different types of product testing. It too should be planned and organized from the beginning of the project.

3.  **Process quality:** Achieved by planning, assessing, and verifying the manufacturing processes used to produce the new product. This should also be planned and organized at the beginning of the project, but it will become more active during the engineering run and pilot production run.

4.  **Project quality control:** An audit of project implementation procedures to monitor, assess, and feed back the control of this specific project in order to fulfil the requirements of design quality, product quality, and process quality.

5.  **Project management audit:** A system audit conducted to review, assess, and improve the project management system itself, in order to assure that all projects are managed systematically, consistently, and effectively. This is a proactive approach to ensure that projects are done right the first time, every time.

## DESIGN QUALITY

The actual design of the product has the greatest influence on its quality. If a product is designed to perform better than the product specification with acceptable manufacturing tolerance, you will have fewer problems during the production phase. Likewise, if a product is designed to barely meet the specifications, then production must perform more tests to ensure that the specifications are being met. This is the basic philosophy for the Six Sigma program. For this reason, design quality is one of the most important elements in new product development projects. To prevent or minimize design quality issues, the team must plan design quality at the outset of the project and integrate the design quality plan with the overall project plan.

At the design quality planning stage, the team should take inputs from the following key areas:

1. **Design rules:** Based on their own past experience, many companies have established their own in-house design rules to guide designers in developing good products. If such rules are unavailable, the team should follow the standard design guidelines published by their suppliers or by professional institutes. The design quality plan should ensure that these design rules are followed; a written report should be prepared to describe exceptions.

2. **Lessons learned from previous projects:** Mistakes made in previous projects, or problems and issues associated with them, are the most valuable lessons for the project team. The design team should review these problems to ensure that they will not be repeated. The design quality plan should ensure that these issues are addressed during design review meetings.

3. **Failure mode and effect analysis (FMEA):** This process was described in Chapter 7. The design quality plan should address the problems and issues identified by the FMEA.

4. **Benchmarking and competitor analysis reports**: These are conducted in order to evaluate the best-in-class products and your competitors' activities. These studies will provide you a clear understanding of the product that the team should develop and reveal the strengths and weaknesses your competitors' products. These findings will serve as a useful reference for the team developing the design quality plan.

*The mistakes made in previous projects (or problems) are most valuable lessons learned.*

5. **Quality data on similar products:** Other important sources of quality data are field failure reports for similar products. The project team should examine customer quality data and devise an action plan to prevent problems from recurring.

6. **Customer requirement specification:** A very important document that specifies clearly the customer requirements and expectations. However, very often this document is not reviewed or is not available for project planning. It is crucial that this document is reviewed and its key points addressed in the project plan.

7. **Quality function deployment (QFD):** A tool widely used in American and Japanese companies to ensure

that customer wants and needs are included in the product planning and development processes. The output of the QFD analysis is a priority list of customer requirements correlated to product parts, processes, and control methods. The design quality plan should ensure that these customer priorities are being reviewed and addressed in the project.

8. **Design evaluation tests (DET):** These tests are usually conducted by the design engineers to evaluate different design options, and normally done in small quantity with mock up or hand-made samples. The design engineers will plan and conduct the tests when necessary, normally in the lowest level of the work breakdown structure (WBS), and details of these tests may not be included in the overall project plan monitored by the project manager. However, as the DET are conducted by design engineers to select design options, the findings should be reviewed at design review meetings.

The output of the design quality plan is a detailed description of key customer requirements, their impact on the project, and actions to be taken by the project team to ensure that these requirements are met. The key information to be included in a design quality plan is summarized in the following section.

## Design Quality Plan

- **Prioritized customer requirements:** Detailed descriptions of top-customer requirements and expectations.
- **Design considerations and criteria for key-customer requirements:** Design criteria that must be met to fulfil these customer requirements.
- **The measurement method for these design criteria:** Methods to measure the effectiveness of the design to fulfil customer requirements.

- **Schedule:** Date that these designs will be completed and verified.
- **Design owner:** Person responsible for the design.
- **Results/findings:** Results of the design verification (at component or subsystem level) at bench-test level, before the system integration.

The design quality plan should be used in every design review meeting. The team should determine whether these key design requirements are being met and, if not, specify corrective actions to be taken. The design quality plan should be updated before the next design review meeting.

## PRODUCT QUALITY–PRODUCT DESIGN VALIDATIONS

The mission of a new product development project is to develop a product that meets specifications, within the time and budget allocated. The purpose of product design validation is to confirm that products have met product specifications.

In general, there are three types of tests:

1. **Design validation tests (DVT):** These tests are usually conducted by quality and reliability engineers to determine whether the product design is ready for production. The DVT should include functional and nonfunctional tests as well as environmental tests. Most companies will test the product not less than one-third of the mean time between failure (MTBF) specification before starting higher volume production. This is a critical decision for production ramp up and should be included in the overall project plan (see Figure 8.1.)

2. **Design maturity tests (DMT):** These tests are also conducted by quality and reliability engineers to confirm that the product design is finalized and ready for production. This is normally the last step before the project enters into the project closeout

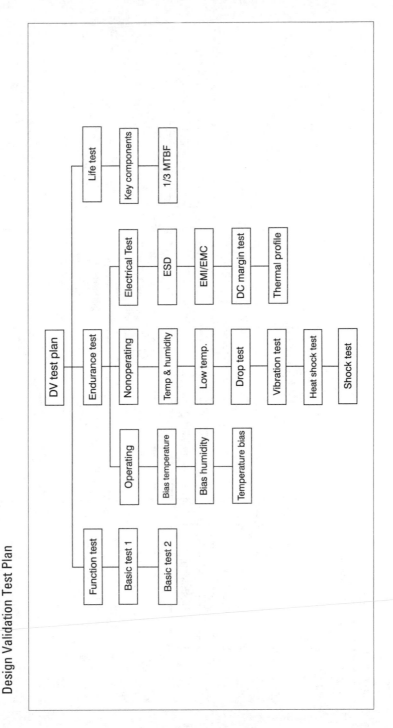

**F I G U R E 8.1**

Design Validation Test Plan

Design Maturity Test Plan

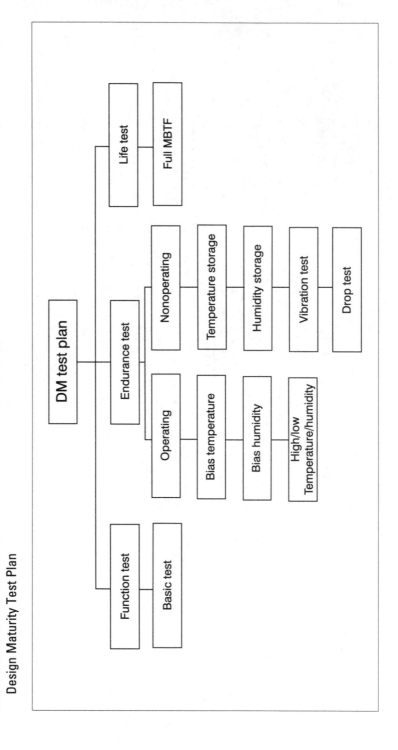

phase. Like the DVT, the DMT should be included as part of the overall project plan (see Figure 8.2).

3. **Ongoing reliability tests:** Once production takes over, they will continue to assess product quality and reliability by conducting regular reliability (environmental) tests. This is normally a part of production tests and not project-related.

## PROCESS QUALITY/PROCESS VERIFICATION TESTS

The process verification test has two purposes: (1) to verify that manufacturing processes will produce the product according to design specifications, and (2) to verify that processes are in place to produce it right the first time. This includes designing the production process to reduce human errors (including applying the principle of foolproofing the process, making it nearly impossible to do the step incorrectly), ensuring equipment repeatability, and reducing the effects of material variability.

To verify that manufacturing processes will produce the product to meet design specifications, the team should first identify the critical design criteria and run a few evaluation samples built in the actual production environment to verify the results. This is commonly referred to as a pre-production run. Normally, this can be done during the engineering run, pilot production, or production trial run. The samples produced during these pre-runs should be analyzed closely before large-scale production begins. The team should review the production yield and test data, analyze the production rejects, and determine whether they are due to manufacturing problems or design-related problems. This is essential to prevent finger-pointing between manufacturing and engineering.

Assuming that the design validation has confirmed that the product will perform as required, process validation must examine four areas that contribute to process problems:

1. **Human error:** The best way to eliminate human error caused by lack of skill or training is to establish an operator training and certification program. In addition, where possible, design the process to be foolproof or mistake-proof, as mentioned above.

2. **Incoming materials quality control:** This is an inspection of raw materials before they are used in production. Normally, incoming inspection takes random samples from incoming batches and tests to see that they meet specifications. However, for critical components, many companies will initially conduct a 100 percent inspection and implement sample inspection only after they are sure that material quality is stabilized.

3. **Machine capability and measurement system:** One of the major process variations is due to machine capability (referred to as CMK) and measurement system variation (equipment repeatability and reproducibility, R&R). The project team should review these two areas for better machines, and test equipment control.

4. **Process capability:** This measures whether the process can produce products consistently across multiple production cycles. Design engineers identify the critical process parameters and monitor these using statistical methods, such as control charts.

## Build a System to Eliminate Human Error

Human error is the most common cause of production error. However, it is important to keep in mind that almost no person wants to do a bad job (except disgruntled employees engaged in deliberate sabotage). In many cases, failure is due to process steps that are not mistake-proof.

The mistake-proof approach is to design the production process so that the operator simply cannot do it wrong. For example, in the printed wiring board assembly operation, using a template that only has a few small windows that will allow the operators to place the components onto the printed circuit board greatly reduces the likelihood of wrong component placement.

No matter what the process, operators must be properly trained to do their jobs. To develop an operator certification program, the team should first identify the process steps that require human judgment and special skills. From this list, the team can then formulate the types of training required to eliminate potential errors. Training ensures that operators understand the processes (manufacturing steps) clearly.

The next step is to assess the operators' knowledge. The final step is to ensure that there is a proper training record and identification of who has attended what types of training.

One of the smartest ways of certifying operators is to have them teach someone else how to do their job. Their ability to do this is convincing evidence that they know the job very well.

## Incoming Quality Control

One of the most basic process control procedures is ensuring that all materials being used in production meet specifications. As stated previously, inspection usually begins with a 100 percent inspection of critical components and changes to sampling after a supplier has proven that they can provide quality components. Nowadays, most companies hold suppliers responsible for the parts' performance at production, thus eliminating incoming inspection. This is called a ship-to-stock program or just-in-time parts. But for new products and new production start-up, most companies minimize their risk by inspecting critical components 100 percent.

## Machine Capability and Measurement System

To build quality into a product, the product design and manufacturing processes play an equally important role.

We previously discussed design quality; now we focus on manufacturing processes.

For all manufacturing processes, machine and test equipment integrity are at the heart of process control. To ensure that the machines and fixtures will produce consistently good products, the machine capability index (CMK) provides clear feedback.

CMK is used to assess the variation of a machine to determine if it meets target performance. For new products, the CMK index is used to specify whether new machines can be released to production. This is only acceptable when the CMK is higher than the target value. The target value is set by the project team or management at the beginning of the project. (For example, the threshold may be "CMK exceeds 1.33," which is equal to four sigma, or "CMK is more than 2," which is equal to six sigma). The machine capability index is also considered as the calculated limits for the process capability index (CPK), as it is impossible for the process to have a higher capability index than the machine producing it. When the target CMK is not met, corrective and improvement actions must be taken before repeating the measurements.

For test equipment control, the team should focus on test equipment repeatability and reproducibility (R&R). When test equipment is used to separate good from bad product, it must be accurate and repeatable. Accuracy means the unit measures correctly. When one unit gives a different measurement than another one, there is a problem with one of them. Repeatability means that the unit consistently gives the same measure of a standard. If equipment measures the same item many times but each time gives a different result, there is a repeatability problem. Usually a test equipment certification group ensures that these issues are addressed.

## Process Capability

A process transforms raw materials into a useful product. A process consists of people, raw materials, procedures, machines, and test equipment. Therefore, process capability is the assessment of the combined performance of these factors in producing a product. A process capability index (CPK) is established by a study conducted on significant product characteristics and process parameters to determine the capability of the process in producing the products in multiple production cycles.

A product can have more than one critical parameter, so, to establish its process capability indices, the team should first determine the list of critical parameters. Once this is done, the team must collect the data for these parameters during the engineering run, production pilot run, and production trial run. These data can be used to compare with the specification limits to calculate the CPK for each critical parameter. Like the CMK, the team should set the target CPK for these critical parameters in advance, and when the target CPK is not met, corrective and improvement actions must be taken before repeating the measurements.

## PROJECT QUALITY CONTROL

The purpose of project quality control is to ensure that all planned activities are carried with positive results. Negative results should trigger corrective actions and proper risk assessment and response. The team should prepare a project quality control plan at the beginning of the project, which should cover all the quality activities required for design quality, quality assurance, and process quality. It should also cover all key project activities, such as design review schedules, FMEA schedules, key management milestone meetings, and risk assessment and response plan review meetings. This plan is not separate from the overall project plan, it is part of it.

The format for the project quality control plan can vary depending on the requirements of a company, but it normally covers the following topics and schedule:

1. **Top-level project milestone plan:** The five major project phases and their respective management milestone meeting schedule.

2. **Product specification release and customer requirement specification review meetings:** These are very important meetings in which the quality team formulates plans for design quality, quality assurance, and process quality.

3. **Design quality plan:** The activities required for achieving design quality. These would include a FMEA schedule, design review schedule, and corrective action plan and tracking system.

4. **Quality assurance plan:** The tests that are required for evaluating product quality, such as the design validation test (DVT) plan and schedule, and the design maturity test (DMT) plan and schedule.

5. **Process quality plan:** The plan for all the machine and test equipment capability studies and process capability studies. This includes the engineering run sample schedule, production trial run schedule, and the production trial run schedule.

6. **Risk management meeting schedules:** Meetings conducted to perform risk identification, assessment, and response planning.

7. **Project problem log review schedule:** A regular meeting to review problems and corrective action status for immediate attention and action.

## Project Management Audit

The project management audit system reviews, assesses, and improves the project management system in order to assure that projects are managed systematically, consistently, and effectively. This is not a project team activity, and is normally conducted by the corporate quality team or by independent project management experts. It is aimed at improving the project management process.

The audit criteria should be based on the individual organization's project management process; however, in general, it should cover the key areas as listed in the *Project Management Body of Knowledge (PMBOK®)*.

There are two project management frameworks:

1. **The project management context:** This covers the environment in which the project is being operated (such as project organization, structure, and reporting) in the project life cycle.

2. **The project management process:** How the project is planned, organized, executed, completed, and closed out. Are process steps standardized and clear to all project team members? How are interactions between project team members and other processes?

There are also nine project management knowledge areas that project managers should attend to for every project:

1. **Project integration management:** This is the process whereby a project manager coordinates various functions within the project and integrates them into a consolidated project plan, which details all activities that must be performed in order to achieve the overall project objective.

2. **Project scope management:** Project scope refers to the project 's boundaries. What *will* be done? What *will not* be done? One cause of project failure is project scope creeping up in small increments, which eventually become very large in total. The project plan should be changed only after considering the impact on scope, and these changes should be approved in writing.

3. **Project time management:** This is a misleading term. The term "time management" conjures images of personal time management for most people–using personal digital assistants, filofax, day-timers, or Franklin Planners. As used in the *PMBOK*, however, it refers to project scheduling, and proficiency in project scheduling can make or break a project.

4. **Project cost management:** This goes without saying. Two cost areas must be managed. One is the cost of running the project, and the other is the cost of producing the new product. There may be tradeoffs to be made between these, and senior management must decide on such exchanges.

5. **Project quality management:** This is the subject of this entire chapter. It means managing the project in such a way that quality goals are achieved.

6. **Project human resources management:** This area of knowledge deals with staffing, developing, and managing human resources to achieve project success. In the United States it also addresses discrimination issues.

7. **Project communication management:** A communication plan is an oft-forgotten aspect of an overall project plan. The team must determine to whom information must be sent, in what format and frequency, and in what mode (written, verbal, formal presentations, etc.)

8. **Project risk management:** Identifying, assessing, and planning for the management of any project risks.

9. **Project procurement management:** This area deals with the procurement of materials, capital equipment, and outside services for a project.

10. **Professional responsibility:** This area deals with the conduct expected of project managers in order to assure that ethics violations are not committed.

## PROJECT MANAGEMENT AUDIT GUIDELINES

The project management audit is an effective method to assess the status of project management in an organization. I do not intend to describe a project management audit in detail, as there is no one way of conducting an audit, and it is outside the scope of this book. However, to the degree that the project management process is itself flawed in some way, you will not be able to accelerate your projects. Remember, *process will always affect task outcomes!*

For that reason, brief guidelines on how to conduct a project audit, together with a checklist for launching an audit in an effective and efficient manner, follow. One benefit of using a standard checklist is to enable a comparison among the audit results for different projects in order to determine if improvements are being made.

The project management audit should be based on following documents:

1.  **The audited organization's project management process or methodology:** One objective of the audit is to determine if the methodology is being followed, and if so, is it effective? If it is not effective then a change to the methodology must be made.

2.  **The *Project Management Body of Knowledge (PMBOK)*:** The audit should determine if the two project management frameworks and nine knowledge areas (as discussed above) are being addressed properly.

3.  **All project documents:** There are many project documents, such as project scope definition, management milestone meeting minutes, the overall project plan, project meeting minutes, and so on that provide information for the audit.

4.  **The corrective action log:** The problems encountered, and their corrective actions and status.

5.  **The related product roadmap:** How projects are being planned, initialized, and executed. This is based on the product strategy or an ad-hoc project.

The project management audit is conducted by examining project documents and conducting interviews with the project manager, project team members, and stakeholders. The detailed checklist follows

| Topic | Knowledge Area | Q/N | Descriptions | Results/ Response | Action Required? |
|---|---|---|---|---|---|
| 1.0 | Project Management Context | 1.1 | Is the project management process defined? | | Yes/ No |
| | | 1.2 | How is the project life cycle defined? | | Yes/ No |
| | | 1.3 | Are the actions in each project life cycle phase defined? (See *PMBOK* 2000, p. 13.) | | Yes/ No |
| | | 1.4 | How is project management reporting? Is the project management structure strong or weak? (See *PMBOK* 2000, pages 19–23.) | | Yes/ No |
| | | 1.5 | Are project stakeholders identified? Who are they, and what are their roles? | | Yes/ No |
| | | 1.6 | Are the standards and regulations related to this project identified and applied? | | Yes/ No |
| 2.0 | Project Management Process | 2.1 | Is the project management process defined? Are the descriptions documented and available to all project team members? | | Yes/ No |
| | | 2.2 | How is the interaction between project team members? | | Yes/ No |
| | | 2.3 | Do they agree with a common project goal? | | Yes/ No |
| | | 2.4 | How are interactions between project team members and other support groups? | | Yes/ No |
| | | 2.5 | What is the assessment of the Initial process? | | Yes/ No |
| | | 2.6 | What is the assessment of the planning process? | | Yes/ No |
| | | 2.7 | What is the assessment of the executing process? | | Yes/ No |
| | | 2.8 | What is the assessment of the controlling process? | | Yes/ No |
| | | 2.9 | What is the assessment of the closing process? | | Yes/ No |

| 3.0 | Project Integration Management | 3.1 | How is the process of project plan development? | | Yes/ No |
|-----|-------------------------------|-----|------------------------------------------------|--|---------|
| | | 3.2 | What is included in the project plan development? | | Yes/ No |
| | | 3.3 | What tools and techniques are used in the project plan development? | | Yes/ No |
| | | 3.4 | How is the project plan communicated to all team members and stakeholders? | | Yes/ No |
| | | 3.5 | Does the project plan provide all stakeholders with sufficient detail? | | Yes/ No |
| | | 3.6 | How is project plan execution? | | Yes/ No |
| | | 3.7 | How is project plan change control? | | Yes/ No |
| | | 3.8 | How are updates to the project plan being communicated to project team members and stakeholders? | | Yes/ No |
| 4.0 | Project Scope Management | 4.1 | What is the process of defining the project scope? | | Yes/ No |
| | | 4.2 | What are the inputs to the project scope? | | Yes/ No |
| | | 4.3 | What techniques and tools are used? | | Yes/ No |
| | | 4.4 | What are the project scope constraints? | | Yes/ No |
| | | 4.5 | Is a work breakdown structure (WBS) template available? | | Yes/ No |
| | | 4.6 | What is the approval process for scope changes? Is the scope change verification in place? | | |
| | | 4.7 | How is scope change controlled? How is it communicated to all team members and stakeholders? | | Yes/ No |

Continued

Continued

| Topic | Knowledge Area | Q/N | Descriptions | Results/ Response | Action Required? |
|-------|----------------|-----|--------------|-------------------|------------------|
| 5.0 | Project Time Management | 5.1 | How is project time being managed, monitored, and controlled? | | Yes/ No |
| | | 5.2 | Are the project activities clearly defined in the WBS? | | Yes/ No |
| | | 5.3 | How is the WBS formatted? Are work elements in units of months, weeks, or days? Does it cover all functions? | | Yes/ No |
| | | 5.4 | Is activity sequencing determined? | | Yes/ No |
| | | 5.5 | What tools and techniques are used for activity sequencing? | | Yes/ No |
| | | 5.6 | How is activity duration estimated? What tools are being used? | | Yes/ No |
| | | 5.7 | What is the process of finalizing the project schedule? | | Yes/ No |
| | | 5.8 | What tools and techniques are used to finalize the project schedule? | | Yes/ No |
| | | 5.9 | Are resources taken into consideration when finalizing the project plan and schedule? | | Yes/ No |
| | | 5.10 | What is the process to compress the time if the duration is considered to be too long? | | Yes/ No |
| | | 5.11 | How will resource shortage issues be addressed? Is the resource-leveling feature of the software being used? | | Yes/ No |
| | | 5.12 | What is the process of schedule control? | | Yes/ No |
| | | 5.13 | How are schedule changes being communicated to all project team members and stakeholders? | | Yes/ No |
| 6.0 | Project Cost Management | 6.1 | What is the process to estimate and plan for the project cost? | | Yes/ No |

| | 6.2 | How are project resources planned and estimated? | | Yes/ No |
|---|---|---|---|---|
| | 6.3 | What inputs and tools are used? | | Yes/ No |
| | 6.4 | What is the process of cost estimation? | | Yes/ No |
| | 6.5 | What inputs and tools are used? | | Yes/ No |
| | 6.6 | How are cost estimates being communicated to management for approval? | | Yes/ No |
| | 6.7 | What is the cost budgeting process? | | Yes/ No |
| | 6.8 | What are the tools and techniques used for cost control? | | Yes/ No |
| | 6.9 | What is the feedback system for cost estimates-versus-actual, and what actions are taken? | | Yes/ No |
| 7.0 | Project Quality Management | | | |
| | 7.1 | How is the quality plan being developed? | | Yes/ No |
| | 7.2 | What major elements are covered in the quality plan? | | Yes/ No |
| | 7.3 | What tools and techniques are being used in design quality? | | Yes/ No |
| | 7.4 | What tools and techniques are being used in product quality assurance? | | Yes/ No |
| | 7.5 | What tools and techniques are being used in process quality? | | Yes/ No |
| | 7.6 | Is the quality control plan for the project adequate? | | Yes/ No |
| | 7.7 | What are the actions taken on the problems and issues raised during the quality check and audit? | | Yes/ No |
| | 7.8 | How effectively is the team addressing quality issues? | | Yes/ No |

Continued

139

Continued

| Topic | Knowledge Area | Q/N | Descriptions | Results/ Response | Action Required? |
|---|---|---|---|---|---|
| 8.0 | Project Human Resource management | 8.1 | How are resource requirements being planned in the project? What is the process? | | Yes/ No |
| | | 8.2 | What tools and techniques are being used? | | Yes/ No |
| | | 8.3 | What is the process to acquire additional project members? What is the approval process? | | Yes/ No |
| | | 8.4 | Is there any plan and action on team development/ team building? | | Yes/ No |
| | | 8.5 | What is the process for monitoring team member performance? How is this being fed back to team members? | | Yes/ No |
| 9.0 | Project Communication Management | 9.1 | What is the project's communication structure? | | Yes/ No |
| | | 9.2 | How is project information being distributed? | | Yes/ No |
| | | 9.3 | What tools and techniques are used? | | Yes/ No |
| | | 9.4 | Is the communication channel effective? | | Yes/ No |
| | | 9.5 | Are project reports timely? Do they reflect true project status? | | Yes/ No |
| 10.0 | Project Risk Management | 10.1 | Is the risk management process defined and being practiced? | | Yes/ No |
| | | 10.2 | What is the risk management process? | | Yes/ No |
| | | 10.3 | What is the assessment of the risk management planning process? | | Yes/ No |

| | | | |
|---|---|---|---|
| | 10.4 | What is the assessment of the risk identification process? | Yes/ No |
| | 10.5 | What is the assessment of the risk assessment process? | Yes/ No |
| | 10.6 | What is the assessment of the risk response and control process? | Yes/ No |
| | 10.7 | What is the assessment of the risk handling and tracking process? | Yes/ No |
| | 10.8 | What is the assessment of the risk management review at the project conceptual phase? | Yes/ No |
| | 10.9 | What is the assessment of the risk management review at the project planning phase? | Yes/ No |
| | 10.10 | What is the assessment of the risk management review at the project Implementation phase? | Yes/ No |
| 11.0 | Project Procurement Management | 11.1 | What is the process of project procurement planning? | Yes/ No |
| | 11.2 | What is the process of supplier selection? | Yes/ No |
| | 11.3 | How are documents or standards provided to suppliers to perform their jobs? | Yes/ No |
| | 11.4 | What system is used to assess supplier performance? | Yes/ No |
| | 11.5 | What is the corrective action system for supplier quality problems and issues? | Yes/ No |
| | 11.6 | What is the system to review the contract with suppliers? | Yes/ No |
| | 11.7 | What is the system to review the quality agreement with supplier? | Yes/ No |

141

# 9

**CHAPTER**

# Manufacturing: Turning a Sample into a Product

*You may be able to produce a hundred samples in your lab; your real challenge is to produce one million in production and make money out of it.*

—Advice to an engineer (source unknown)

The most critical moment in any new product development is when it enters production. Let's face it: if you have a great product but you cannot produce it, you really do not have a product. If your engineers can make samples in the lab but your production facility has great difficulty manufacturing the product in high volume, it will not be a winning product for you. The key is to balance the requirements between time-to-market and mass-production. However, this balance

Why are people NOT cooperating?

can be very difficult to achieve and often leads to major conflicts between R&D and manufacturing.

It is no secret that many companies struggle to resolve the conflict between these two functions. This conflict often hurts the company badly, as products may miss the market introduction window. There are always two sides to a story, but regardless of this, the fact is that a late product hurts everyone in the company.

The problem is, why are people not cooperating? One answer lies in the basic organizational structure and performance measurements. In their book, *Developing Products in Half the Time*, the authors summarize this conflict in a very simple way: "It is not surprising that manufacturing often sees new products as a problem rather than a benefit. After all, they get measured on the basis of monthly shipments and gross margins. . . . There is simply very little short-term incentive for most manufacturing organizations to support new products" (Smith & Reinertsen, 1998).

From the development function point of view, they could design a product that will cover every possible problem in production, but to do so would require so much time that, by the time it is released, it would already be obsolete. So the real question is: What is good enough for production and how do you achieve it? Smith and Reinertsen suggest the following actions to address this conflict:

1. **Create opportunities for overlapping:** "Manufacturing is forced to be involved from the beginning. If the manufacturing people join the team full-time from the beginning, they will either have to work on engineering or marketing tasks, or identify opportunities for overlap so they can begin work on manufacturing tasks, even if this must be done with only partial information."

2. **Change incentives for manufacturing:** This is a long-term approach that gives credits and incentives to manufacturing for introducing new products.

3. **Provide a champion for new products in the factory:** This champion should be from manufacturing, but reports to development during product development and introduction. Because he is from manufacturing, he will have more credibility and influence within the factory than would someone from development.

4. **Members of the development team should spend real time on the factory floor:** When the team spends time to understand production processes, they get valuable manufacturing experience that should go into product design. They also establish contacts and relationships with manufacturing for future process and equipment development discussion.

The suggestions outlined by Smith and Reinertsen are good tactical ones. The process enables manufacturing to get more involved in the new product development process, but it does not resolve the fundamental conflict. Some questions remain:

1. How do you get manufacturing interested in producing a new product?

2. How can manufacturing become a willing partner for new product introduction?

3. What is in it for the head of manufacturing?

4. What would you do if you were the leader of these two functions?

When Louis Wong was an operations manager for a disk drive company, his division manager always told him, "You must keep your organization lean and mean. But your engineering people must be capable. They must be able to handle all types of product and process problems. Nobody will disagree with you that quality is the most important job, but how to solve a quality problem is the heart of the issue. Your engineering people must have a can-do and will-do attitude. The question is, how do you instill this attitude in manufacturing for new product introduction?"

Clearly, manufacturing has no function if they have no products to build, and since all products become obsolete over time, unless there is a steady flow of new products they will eventually find themselves jobless. If they understand this, they will fight to take new products into production. They must also be capable of handling problems after they begin mass production. To achieve this goal, some possible strategies follow:

1. Create competition among factories if you have them. The factory that can produce the new product at lowest cost and highest quality "wins" the job.

2. Manufacturing can/will make money from new product introduction.

3. Process and equipment development should report to manufacturing.

4. Enable manufacturing with a strong advance engineering team.

## Creating Competition among Factories

When Wong was a regional program manager for a semiconductor company in Singapore, the company would hold an "Annual Operations Plan" meeting that would decide that year's operational budget and what products to allocate to which factory in Asia Pacific. Plant managers would first present their plans, and value-added activities that they could implement, and identify products they would like to produce. Everyone was eager to take on more new products, of course, along with the investment and new technology that attends them. This was a great motivation for the factories. They all knew very well that if they did not get new products, the factory would run out of work and have overcapacity. In fact, the net result was that not a single plant manager complained about problems with any new products they had taken on previously; they only wanted more new products, regardless of what would happen during production later on.

If you have only one factory, you could invite your subcontractors into the discussion. The objective is to make them willing partners. They should be the ones telling you that they want to take on new products. Following is a simple process for achieving this result:

1.  Before the project starts, invite your project manager to present a project overview to your factory and/or subcontractor representatives to enable them to understand the project scope, the target quantity, target production schedule, target factory price, and resources required to support this project.

2.  Give them one or two weeks to think and plan. They must review the impact of this project on their factory and come back with a proposal that should cover the target factory prices and full-time resources they will provide to support this project.

3.  A committee chaired by the manufacturing manager should review their proposals, and then decide who gets this job. Let the best proposal win.

The outcome of this process is a firm commitment from the factory. At the same time, enabling the manufacturing people who are assigned to this project will create a strong bond between them and the project team. Such team spirit from the factory is very important to the project, as it will smooth over problems and difficulties later on. Since it is now an achievement for the factory to be awarded a new product (after all, they have to be better than other factories), they have to do everything possible to win the work. The manufacturing boss will also do everything possible to make this happen, because his or her own reputation is at stake (as he or she chairs the selection committee.)

## Capture the True Cost of Introducing a New Product

Even given a commitment from manufacturing, if they feel they are treated unfairly it will evaporate. The factory must not be penalized for something over which they have no control. Therefore, it is essential to establish a cost center in the factory to capture all new product introduction costs and charge them back to development. This is not just for accounting purposes, but to capture the true development costs for better future planning and business case justification. In most new product justifications, the development cost does not cover the scrap cost, labor cost, and equipment downtime during prototype and pilot production stages. Initial production is normally not as efficient as the final production run, after the learning curve has been traversed. Under normal conditions, production has to shoulder all these additional costs, which adversely affects their overall performance. Having the new cost center record these costs puts them in the right perspective.

It's essential to give credit to the factory if they drive the various costs below the introduction targets. Each project will have a budget for sample run, scrap cost, equipment cost, and so on. If the factory team helps to reduce costs in the actual prototype manufacture, sample build, and pilot produc-

*Capture the true costs of introducing a new product.*

tion, they deserve credit. In the costing system, if production spends less than the development target budget, it should be positive IFO (income from operations) for the factory—which gives them incentive, because they can be rewarded when they do well. If they spend over the target, the additional cost should be shared with development.

The details of this scheme can be worked out based on the company's finance and accounting system, but the concept is that the project team should have a budget for all the new product introduction costs as part of the business case justification. The cost for prototype and pilot production should be planned and allocated to the factory that is doing

the job. Of course, for the company, it is just a left pocket/
right pocket issue, but it provides measures that help to moti-
vate the factory to excel in the project team in order to benefit
from this new product introduction.

## Process and Equipment Development Ownership

Traditionally, process and equipment development are considered development functions. Since manufacturing is the final customer for the process and equipment, development
should involve manufacturing during the design stage. However, manufacturing may feel that it is too early for them to
get involved or, due to other pressing production problems,
they may shy away from the development process. On the
other hand, because the factory is often far from the development center, engineers may feel that they will start the work
first and talk to the factory later. In the end, the discussion
never takes place.

Ownership is another problem. Development managers
always feel they are responsible for designing new products,
but they do not feel strongly that they should own the manufacturing process or equipment development. After all, they design products. It is manufacturing's responsibility to figure out
how to build them. You may think this wrong, but it is the per-
ception of the development mangers and it is hard to change.

In the case of production, they have long-term interests
in the process and equipment design. When equipment is developed, it will be difficult for them to create a budget to replace that equipment as it wears out. As such, production has
more reasons to own the process and equipment development. Therefore, we suggest that the process and equipment
development function should report to manufacturing; that
is, the process development council and equipment development council should report to manufacturing instead of reporting to development or the innovation department. This
ensures that the process and equipment development processes have a direct link to manufacturing. When the produc-

tion team is involved directly in the project, they get more direct feedback from production on the process and equipment before it is finalized for prototype build and pilot production. During the product development phase, a full-time manufacturing engineer should work with the project team and report to the project manager. The engineer should actively participate in project planning and prepare the team for prototype building and a trial-run schedule. He/she should also advocate the decision to start up production, and communicate this readiness to manufacturing.

## Enable Manufacturing with a Strong Advance-Engineering Team

Ask yourself: If I were the development manager, would I want a strong manufacturing partner that resolves all the product or process problems after the product development stage, or a weak manufacturing group that always needs help to resolve product or process problems after the product is introduced?

This is not an easy question to answer, because there are pros and cons. Still, a strong and capable manufacturing department that will resolve most production problems before asking for support is preferable. When they lack this capability, you often find that new product development personnel (call that "project resources") are pulled off the job to solve urgent product problems, thus delaying development of new products. The net result is that the deadline for the new product does not change, and when these engineers come back to the job they are forced to rush to finish their designs, thus creating another product with design flaws. The circle is a vicious one, and has no end as long as this system prevails.

There are certainly times when development engineers will have to solve problems with products already in the field, but keep this to a minimum if you want to accelerate new product development. If you think the cost of supporting such a group is high, consider the cost of losing customers because of recurring problems with product design quality!

When you place the process and equipment development under manufacturing, there is another benefit—the process and equipment development teams will better communicate with the manufacturing engineering team, and there will be cross-fertilization between the groups. The development team will know more about the process and equipment problems in a real production environment, while the production team will learn more about the process and equipment design. This benefits and strengthens both teams in the long run.

## THE ONE-TEAM CONCEPT

Almost any project expert will tell you that you must have only one team for a project, and that all team members should report to just one project manager. However, in many cases, because manufacturing is located at a distance from the development center, the site leader and team members are almost certain to have their own normal duties on top of their project activities. They will usually report to a functional boss on a solid-line basis and to the project manager on a dotted line. This is always the source of difficulties, conflicts and problems.

While it may be difficult to change this arrangement, there is another way to manage. The site project leader and team members should report directly to the development project manager (hereafter simply called the project manager). If there is any additional duty that they can perform without affecting project progress, site management should communicate this request to the project manager for approval. Only when the project manager agrees with the request are the site members permitted to carry out those duties. This may sound like simple common sense, but many organizations have more than one project leader, all reporting to different bosses and claiming that they still report to the project manager. Under these conditions, the project manager has little or no control of the activities of off-site personnel, which makes tracking, monitoring, and controlling the project impossible. In view of geographical location differences, the line of command and reporting is very critical for project success.

When implementing the above strategy, to win support from manufacturing, the site manager should change the line of reporting as suggested once the factory is committed to the project. He or she also should propose a resource allocation plan, thus providing a clear mandate to the project manager to execute the project.

## Cooperative Attitude

The most important objective of these actions is to foster a cooperative attitude. The development and manufacturing teams must work closely, as they are members of one team.

An old story illustrates this point. A merchant once set forth on a journey to a mountainous region. He brought along many goods, an old donkey, a young mule, and a horse. He rode the horse and loaded his goods on the other two animals. The young mule looked quite strong, so he loaded most of his heavy goods on it and put only some light goods on the old donkey. At first the young mule carried his load with ease, but when he began to ascend the steep path of the mountain, his load became too much for him to bear. He began to travel with great pain.

The young mule then spoke to the old donkey in the hope that he would help him lighten his load. But the donkey paid little attention to his request. He then turned to the horse hoping he could help him instead. But the horse said to the mule, "I am carrying the master, putting some goods on my back will make the master very uncomfortable." So the horse too turned down the young mule's request and carried on.

Not long afterward, the young mule dropped dead under his heavy burden. Not knowing what else to do, the man placed all the goods carried by the mule on the donkey and the horse and continued to ride the horse for the rest of his journey.

The donkey and the horse, groaning beneath their heavy burdens, said to themselves, "We deserve this punishment. If we had only been willing to assist the mule a little, he wouldn't have died and we wouldn't be carrying his load."

The leader's role is to foster a cooperative attitude between development and manufacturing. If the leader is unwilling to promote this cooperative working attitude, the company—like the mule—will fall, and everyone will suffer.

## The Role of Site Project Manager

When a product is initiated in the development center but the manufacturing center is at a different site, a site project manager must be assigned to the manufacturing center. The objective is to involve the manufacturing site at the outset of the project and ensure that the industrial inputs are taken into consideration when developing the new product. This is especially important when the development center is utilizing a new platform or technology. When a product is being developed in the mass-manufacturing center, the project manager may combine both roles. One of the site project manager's most important roles is bridging the differences between the development center and manufacturing.

## The Development Project Manager

The development project manager (again, simply called project manager hereafter) is responsible for the overall project from the concept stage through the closeout stage. He or she ensures the project's success.

The project manager's roles and responsibilities are:

1. **Establish project deliverables (product function and features, quality, time, and cost):** The project

manager should define and finalize project deliverables based on the defined project scope. He or she should review these deliverables with the project sponsor and stakeholders to secure their agreement up front in order to minimize changes during the project execution stage.

2. **Overall project planning and execution:** The project manager should establish and oversee the overall project plan, and work with the subteam leaders to support it.

3. **Resource planning and execution:** While management should allocate full-time core-team members to the project team, the project manager should follow up to ensure that the resources are available according to the project plan.

4. **Budget control and reporting:** The project manager should control project expenditures and report progress to management.

5. **Project business case review and reporting:** During project execution, the project manager should update the project business case and report major changes to management.

6. **Communication with stakeholders:** One of the major roles for the project manager is to keep an open communication channel with project stakeholders. Should there be major changes, the project manager should try to gain consensus from the stakeholders and should strive to avoid any surprises.

7. **Communication with key customers:** The project manager should continue the ongoing communication with key customers and ensure that customers are aware of project progress and changes.

8. **Communication with key suppliers and subcontractors:** Should there be any changes in the project; the project manager should ensure that they are communicated to suppliers and subcontractors. This

is to ensure that suppliers are kept up to date on changes and to avoid miscommunications.

9. **Risk assessment and preventive actions:** An important role for the project manager is to continuously assess risks and ensure that proper preventive actions are taken.

10. **Project progress and reporting to management:** The project manager should report project progress to management and highlight major problems that require management attention.

## Site Project Manager Roles and Responsibilities

The site project manager's primary job is to support the project manager to ensure that industrial requirements and inputs are considered at the beginning of the project and are implemented during its execution. The site project manager will also lead site implementation work during the project Implementation stage. The site project manager will also ensure that the product improvement team (PIT) is established to take over the product after the project closeout stage. His or her major roles and responsibilities are:

1. Participate in and contribute to project planning and evaluate the project plan to ensure that manufacturing interests are addressed. This is critical, as early participation of the industrial team will ensure that the project manager has adequate industrial inputs to consider.

2. Detailed project planning relating to site activities per the project master plan, and the plan's execution at the site. Monitor and control the site project implementation according to the project master plan.

3. Project budget for site activities (including production equipment and production line budget, etc.).

Site budget control is one the site project manager's most important responsibilities.

4. Ensure that adequate site resources are allocated for the project. Raise the red flag when resources problems are not resolved.

5. Take the lead for site trial-run activities (production evaluation run before starting production), results, and reporting. Communicate the results, findings, issues, and actions to the project manager.

6. Ensure that the infrastructure (people, equipment, etc.) is ready for the trial run. Also responsible for ensuring that the normal trial-run parts are available. The project manager is responsible for any unique/special parts for the trial run.

7. Site production ramp-up plan and its capacity; e.g., line layout, setup, molds, equipment, and training.

8. Lead the project when it is implemented in production. This is a joint responsibility with the project manager to ensure successful site implementation.

9. Exchange site project progress and overall project progress with the project manager in a timely manner.

# Competence Building
# through Learning

*Core competencies are the collective learning in the organization, especially how to coordinate diverse production skills and integrate multiple streams of technologies. . . . The real sources of advantage are to be found in management's ability to consolidate the competencies that empower individual businesses to adapt quickly to changing opportunities.*

— Prahalad and Hamel

**N**o doubt many of you read *The Tortoise and the Hare* when you were children. Lately there has been a new version of this classic fable circulating on the Internet. Here is how it goes:

*If you take too long to finish a new product, it may be obsolete.*

Once upon a time a tortoise and a hare had an argument about who was faster. They decided to settle the argument with a race. They agreed on a route and started the race. The hare shot ahead and ran briskly for some time. Then, seeing that he was far ahead of the tortoise, the hare decided he could sit under a tree for a while and relax before continuing the race. Soon he fell asleep. The tortoise, plodding on, overtook him and finished the race, emerging as the undisputed champion. The hare woke up and realized that he'd lost the race.

The moral of the story is that even if you are better today; it does not guarantee your future success. You cannot idle, or else your competitors will catch up and overtake you. Dr. Deming said that there are two kinds of companies, those that are getting better and those that are dying. If you're standing still, you're dying; you just don't know it yet.

Fortunately, one failure does not usually mean the end of the line (although there are clear exceptions). Most of the time, the race will continue. This is the added modern twist to the old story.

The hare was disappointed at losing the race and he did some soul-searching. He realized that he'd lost the race only because he had been overconfident, careless, and slack. If he had not taken things for granted there's no way the tortoise could have beaten him. So he challenged the tortoise to another race. The tortoise agreed. This time, the hare went all out and ran without stopping, from start to finish, and he won by several miles.

What is the moral of the story? When you lose a battle, it is not the end of the war. You need to know why you failed, and determine your core competence and how to use it to your advantage.

But the story doesn't end here either.

The tortoise did some thinking this time, and realized that there's no way he could beat the hare in this race. He thought for a while, and then challenged the hare to another race, but on a different route. The hare agreed. In keeping with his self-made commitment to be consistently fast, the hare took off and ran at top speed until he came to a broad river. The finish line was a couple of kilometers on the other side of the river.

The hare sat there wondering what to do. In the meantime the tortoise trundled along, got into the river, swam to the opposite bank, continued walking and finished the race.

Now what is the moral of the story?

First: identify your core competency and then change the playing field to suit it. In a competitive market, you must use your competence to your advantage to build the core products that will give your customers desired value and service.

But wait—the story is not yet ended!

By this time the hare and the tortoise had become pretty good friends and they did some thinking together. Both realized that their last race could have been run much faster. So they decided to race again, as a team—against time. Their goal was to beat their respective best times. They started off with the hare carrying the tortoise to the riverbank. There, the tortoise took over and swam across with the hare on his back. On the opposite bank, the hare again carried the tortoise and they reached the finish line together. This time both of them are winners. They beat their own best times *when they worked together as a team.* Both felt a greater sense of satisfaction than they had felt earlier.

The moral of the story now?

It's good to be individually brilliant and to have strong competencies; but unless you are able to work as a team harnessing each other's core competencies, you will always perform below par because there will be situations in which you will do poorly and someone else will do well. Teamwork is mainly about utilizing the right competence at the right time and at the right place. When the team has a common goal, its strength is equal to the sum of its competencies. It is always more powerful than any single individual.

There are more lessons to be learned from this story.

Note that neither the hare nor the tortoise gave up after failures. The hare decided to work harder and put in more effort after his failure. The tortoise changed his strategy because he was already working as hard as he could. In life, when faced with failure, sometimes it is appropriate to work harder and put in more effort. Sometimes it is appropriate to change strategy and try something different. And sometimes it is appropriate to do both.

The hare and the tortoise also learned another valuable lesson. When they quit competing against each other and started cooperating, they achieved far better results. Just as we discussed in Chapter 9, if manufacturing and development will work as a team, they can achieve much faster time-to-market and volume-to-market, which makes everyone in the company a winner. The point is that both hare and tortoise learned from their mistakes and found new ways to counter their problems.

## THE PROJECT AS THE PLAYING FIELD FOR COMPETENCE DEVELOPMENT

One of the most important factors in a project's success is the competency of team members. Any project manager will tell you that he or she will require a very competent team to

*Project participation is in fact the best training.*

solve those unexpected project problems! The project manager has no time to train people—they are expected to know their jobs. A project should not be a training ground for its members.

Yet, for many, project participation is in fact the best training ground. While all projects need capable members, a project is also a great opportunity to develop competencies. It's called learning by doing. It takes place during project implementation, as well as at the end of the project.

How can we develop competencies while executing a project? As Prahalad and Hamel suggest, "Core competencies are the collective learning in the organization," meaning that the best place for team learning is during project execution. The team learns what is right and what is missing, and they enhance their capability—thus increasing their competencies as a whole. Think of this as a plan-do-check-act

**F I G U R E   10.1**

PDCA Cycle

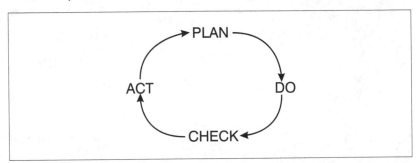

(PDCA) cycle. When the project team launches (plan), they encounter new problems (do). They find a solution (check). They internalize it and gain a new capability (act), and this improvement cycle continues (see Figure 10.1).

The critical issue is how to share this knowledge beyond the project boundary. Many companies are unsuccessful in sharing lessons learned from mistakes. Only problem solving can enhance team competencies. It is vital that this lesson permeates the entire organization, that those who are the "right" people to know this lesson learn it. Organizational learning means preventing problems, not just by one person but by the whole organization.

"Organizations learn only through individuals who learn. Individual learning does not guarantee organizational learning. But without it no organizational learning occurs" (Senge, 1990). Because team learning occurs basically through members who learn from their problems and mistakes, it is essential to document these processes and formally share them with others. And the best way to internalize a new skill is by teaching it and interacting with learners. Ongoing presentations on project problems and solutions will enhance the company's overall competencies.

Remember, no project is ever a complete failure. It can always be used as a bad example!

# REFERENCES AND READING LIST

Ackoff, Russell. *Ackoff's Fables: Irreverent Reflections on Business and Bureaucracy.* New York: Wiley, 1991.

Ackoff, Russell. *The Art of Problem Solving.* New York: Wiley, 1978.

Ackoff, Russell. *Creating the Corporate Future.* New York: Wiley, 1981.

Ackoff, Russell. *The Democratic Corporation.* New York: Oxford University Press, 1994.

Adams, James L. *Conceptual Blockbusting: A Guide to Better Ideas,* Second Edition. New York: W. W. Norton, 1979.

Adams, John D., Editor. *Transforming Leadership: From Vision to Results.* Alexandria, VA: Miles River Press, 1986.

Ailes, Roger. *You Are the Message: Secrets of the Master Communicators.* Homewood, IL: Dow Jones-Irwin, 1988.

Albrecht, Karl. *The Northbound Train.* New York: AMACOM, 1994.

Archibald, R. D., and R. L. Villoria. *Network-based Management Systems (Pert/CPM).* New York: Wiley, 1967.

Argyris, Chris. *Overcoming Organizational Defenses: Facilitating Organizational Learning.* Boston: Allyn and Bacon, 1990.

Axelrod, Robert. *The Evolution of Cooperation.* New York: Basic Books, 1984.

Barker, Joel A. *Future Edge.* New York: William Morrow, 1992.

Barker, Joel A. *Wealth, Innovation & Diversity*. Videotape. Carlsbad, CA: CRM Learning, 2000.

Bauer, Eugene E. *Boeing: The First Century*. Enumclaw, Washington: TABA Publishing, 2000.

Bedi, Hari. *Understanding the Asian Manager*. Singapore: Heinemann Asia, 1992.

Beer, Stafford. *Brain of the Firm*, Second Edition. New York: Wiley, 1981.

Bennis, Warren G. *Managing the Dream: Reflections on Leadership and Change*. Cambridge, MA: Perseus, 2000.

Bennis, Warren G., and Burt Nanus. *Leaders: The Strategies for Taking Charge*. New York: Harper & Row, 1985.

Benveniste, Guy. *Mastering the Politics of Planning*. San Francisco: Jossey-Bass, 1989.

Barnhart, Robert K. *The Barnhart Concise Dictionary of Etymology: The Origins of American English Words*. New York: HarperCollins, 1995.

Blanchard, Benjamin S. *Engineering Organization and Management*. Englewood Cliffs, NJ: Prentice-Hall, 1976.

Blake, Robert, and Jane Mouton. *The Managerial Grid*. Houston: Gulf Publishing, 1964.

Block, Peter. *The Empowered Manager*, Second Edition. San Francisco: Jossey-Bass, 2000.

Bodanis, David. *E=mc²: A Biography of the World's Most Famous Equation*. New York: Walker & Company, 2000.

Brooks, F. P. *The Mythical Man-Month: Essays on Software Engineering*. Reading, MA: Addison-Wesley, 1975.

Bunker, Barbara Benedict, and Alban, Billie T. *Large Group Interventions: Engaging the Whole System for Rapid Change*. San Francisco: Jossey-Bass, 1997.

Burns, James McGregor. *Leadership*. New York: Harper & Row, 1978.

Buzan, Tony. *The Mind Map Book*. New York: NAL/Dutton, 1996.

Carlzon, Jan. *Moments of Truth*. New York: Perennial, 1987.

Chen, Yanping, and Francis N. Arko. *Principles of Contracting for Project Management*. Arlington, VA: UMT Press, 2003

Cialdini, Robert B. *Influence: The Power of Persuasion,* Revised Edition. New York: Quill, 1993.

Cleland, David I., and William R. King, Editors. *Project Management Handbook.* New York: Van Nostrand Reinhold, 1983.

Collins, Jim. *Good to Great.* New York: HarperCollins, 2001.

Covey, Stephen. *The 7 Habits of Highly Effective People.* New York: Fireside Books, 1989.

Crosby, Philip B. *Quality Is Free.* New York: McGraw-Hill, 1980.

de Bono, Edward. *New Think.* New York: Avon Books, 1971.

de Bono, Edward. *Serious Creativity.* New York: Harper, 1992.

de Bono, Edward. *Six Thinking Hats.* Boston: Little, Brown & Co., 1985.

Deming, Edwards. *Out of the Crisis.* Cambridge, MA: Massachusetts Institute of Technology, 1986.

Dimancescu, Dan. *The Seamless Enterprise: Making Cross-Functional Management Work.* New York: Harper, 1992.

Downs, Alan. *Corporate Executions: The Ugly Truth about Layoffs: How Corporate Greed Is Shattering Lives, Companies, and Communities.* New York: AMACOM, 1995.

Drucker, Peter F. *Management: Tasks, Responsibilities, Practices.* New York: Harper & Row, 1973, 1974.

Dyer, Wayne. *You'll See It When You Believe It.* New York: Avon Books, 1989.

Eisenstein, Paul A. "How Toyota's Kentucky Operations Mix People, Processes to Be Best." *Investor's Business Daily,* 12/4/2000.

Firth, Robert. *Project Risk Management.* Institute of Systems Science, 1999.

Fleming, Q. W. *Cost/Schedule Control Systems Criteria.* Chicago: Probus, 1988.

Fleming, Quentin W., and Koppelman, Joel M. *Earned Value Project Management.* Upper Darby, PA: Project Management Institute, 1996.

Fortune, Joyce, and Geoff Peters. *Learning from Failure: The Systems Approach.* Chichester, England: Wiley, 1998.

Frame, J. Davidson. *Managing Projects in Organizations*. San Francisco: Jossey-Bass, 1995.

Frame, J. Davidson. *The New Project Management*, Second Edition. San Francisco: Jossey-Bass, 2002.

Frame, J. Davidson. *Project Finance: Tools and Techniques*. Arlington, VA: UMT Press, 2003.

Frankl, Viktor. *Man's Search for Meaning,* Third. Edition. New York: Touchstone, 1984.

Freiberg, Kevin, and Jackie Freiberg. *Nuts! Southwest Airlines' Crazy Recipe for Business and Personal Success*. New York: Broadway Books, 1996.

Gardner, Howard. *Frames of Mind: The Theory of Multiple Intelligences*. New York: Basic Books, 1993.

Garten, Jeffrey E. *The Mind of the C.E.O.* New York: Basic Books, 2001.

Gause, Donald, and Gerald Weinberg. *Exploring Requirements: Quality before Design*. New York: Dorset House Publishing, 1989.

Goldratt, Eliyahu M. *Critical Chain*. Great Barrington, MA: The North River Press, 1997.

Graham, Robert J. and Randall L. Englund. *Creating an Environment for Successful Projects*. San Francisco: Jossey-Bass, 1997.

Hammer, Michael, and James Champy. *Reengineering the Corporation*. New York: Harper Business, 1993.

Hancock, Graham. *Fingerprints of the Gods*. New York: Crown, 1995.

Harling, Christopher J. Senior Management Workshop for Philips, 2001.

Harry, Mikel, and Richard Schroeder. *Six Sigma: The Breakthrough Management Strategy Revolutionizing the World's Top Corporations*. New York: Currency, 2000.

Harvey, Jerry B. *The Abilene Paradox and Other Meditations on Management*. San Diego: University Associates, 1988.

Heller, Robert. *Achieving Excellence*. New York: DK Publishing, 1999.

Heller, Robert, and Tim Hindle. *Essential Manager's Manual*. New York: DK Publishing, 1998.

Herrmann, Ned. *The Creative Brain*. Lake Lure, NC: Brain Books, 1995.

Herrmann, Ned. *The Whole Brain Business Book*. New York: McGraw-Hill, 1996.

Hersey, Paul, and Kenneth Blanchard. *Management of Organizational Behavior: Utilizing Human Resources*, Fourth Edition. Englewood Cliffs, NJ: Prentice-Hall, 1981.

Hiebeler, Robert, Thomas Kelly, and Charles Ketteman. *Best Practices: Building Your Business with Customer-Focused Solutions*. New York: Simon and Schuster, 1998.

Highsmith, III, James A. *Adaptive Software Development*. New York: Dorset House, 2000.

Ittner, Christopher D., and David F. Larckner. "A Bigger Yardstick for Company Performance." London: *The Financial Times*, 10/16/2000.

Janis, Irving, and Leon Mann. *Decision Making*. New York: The Free Press, 1977.

Johnson, Spencer. *Who Moved My Cheese?* New York: G. P. Putnam's Sons, 1998.

Jones, Russell A. *Self-Fulfilling Prophecies*. Hillsdale, NJ: Lawrence Erlbaum, 1977.

Kayser, Tom. *Mining Group Gold*. New York: McGraw-Hill, 1995.

Keane. *Productivity Management: Keane's Project Management Approach for Systems Development*, Second Edition. Boston: Keane Associates (800-239-0296)

Keirsey, David. *Please Understand Me II*. Del Mar, CA: Prometheus Nemesis Book Company, 1998.

Kepner, Charles H., and Benjamin B. Tregoe. *The Rational Manager*. Princeton, NJ: Kepner-Tregoe, Inc., 1965.

Kerzner, Harold. *In Search of Excellence in Project Management*. New York: Van Nostrand, 1998.

Kerzner, Harold. *Project Management: A Systems Approach to Planning, Scheduling, and Controlling*, Fifth Edition. New York: Van Nostrand, 1995.

Kiemele, Mark J., and Stephen R. Schmidt. *Basic Statistics. Tools for Continuous Improvement*, Third Edition. Colorado Springs, CO: Air Academy Press, 1993.

Knight, James A. *Value-Based Management: Developing a Systematic Approach to Creating Shareholder Value*. New York: McGraw-Hill, 1998.

Knowles, Malcolm. *Self-Directed Learning*. New York: Association Press, 1975.

Koch, Richard. *The 80/20 Principle*. New York: Doubleday, 1998.

Kopelman, Orion. "Do It Right the First Time and Develop Products in Half the Time!" Washington, D.C.: *ProjectWorld*, Summer 1996.

Kouzes, James M., and Barry Z. Posner. *The Leadership Challenge: How to Get Extraordinary Things Done in Organizations*. San Francisco: Jossey-Bass, 1987.

Kuhn, Thomas. *The Structure of Scientific Revolutions*. Chicago: University of Chicago Press, 1970.

Leider, Richard J. *Life Skills: Taking Charge of Your Personal and Professional Growth*. Paramus, NJ: Prentice Hall, 1994.

Leider, Richard J. *The Power of Purpose: Creating Meaning in Your Life and Work*. San Francisco: Berrett Koehler, 1997.

Lerner, Michael. *The Politics of Meaning*. Reading, MA: Addison-Wesley, 1996.

Lewis, James. *Fundamentals of Project Management*, Second Edition. New York: AMACOM, 2001.

Lewis, James P. *Mastering Project Management*. New York: McGraw-Hill, 1998.

Lewis, James P. "Project Fast-Tracking and Evaluation." Presentation to PMI Singapore Chapter members, 3/12/2003.

Lewis, James P. *Project Leadership*. New York: McGraw-Hill, 2002.

Lewis, James P. *Project Planning, Scheduling and Control*, Third Edition. New York: McGraw-Hill, 2000.

Lewis, James P. *The Project Manager's Desk Reference*, Second Edition. New York: McGraw-Hill, 2000.

Lewis, James P. *The Project Manager's Pocket Survival Guide*. New York: McGraw-Hill, 2003.

Lewis, James P. *Team-Based Project Management*. New York: AMACOM, 1997.

Lewis, James P. *Working Together*. New York: McGraw-Hill, 2002.

MacMillan, Ian C., and Rita Gunther. "Corporate Ventures: Maximising Gains." London: *Financial Times*, 10/16/2000.

Madden, Jerry. *100 Rules for Project Managers*. NASA, 7/9/1996.

Maidique, Modesto, and Billie Jo Zirger. *The New Product Learning Cycle*. Research Policy. (Cited in Peters, 1987.)

Maier, Norman R. F. *Psychology in Industry*. Boston: Houghton Mifflin, 1955.

Maloney, Lawrence D. "For the Love of Flying." *Design News*, vol. 51, number 5, 3/4/1996.

March, James, and Herbert Simon. *Organizations*. New York: Wiley, 1966.

Maslow, Abraham. *Motivation and Personality*, Second Edition. New York: Harper & Row, 1970.

McCartney, Scott. "Out of the Blue. How Two Pacific Nations Became Oceanic Aces of Air-Traffic Control." *The Wall Street Journal*, Friday, 12/29/2000.

McClelland, David. *Power: The Inner Experience*. New York: Halsted Press, 1975.

McGraw, Phillip. *Life Strategies: Doing What Works, Doing What Matters*. New York, Hyperion, 1999.

Michalko, Michael. *Thinkertoys*. Berkeley, CA: Ten Speed Press, 1995.

Miller, William C. *The Creative Edge: Fostering Innovation Where You Work*. Reading, MA: Addison-Wesley, 1986.

Mintzberg, Henry. *Mintzberg on Management*. New York: The Free Press, 1989.

Moder, Joseph J., Cecil R. Phillips, and Edward W. Davis. *Project Management with Cpm, Pert, and Precedence Diagramming*, Third Edition. New York: Van Nostrand, 1983.

Morrison, Terri, Wayne A. Conaway, and George A. Borden. *Kiss, Bow, or Shake Hands*. Holbrook, MA: Adams Media Corporation, 1994.

Mouzelis, N. P. "Bureaucracy," *The New Encyclopaedia Britannica*, Fifteenth Edition. Macropaedia 3 (1974).

Nadler, Gerald, and Shozo Hibino. *Breakthrough Thinking*. Rocklin, CA: Prima Publishing, 1990.

Nellore, Rajesh. "R&D Structures to Keep the Focus on Products." London: *Financial Times*, 12/11/2000.

von Oech, Roger. *A Whack on the Side of the Head*. New York: Warner, 1983.

von Oech, Roger. *A Kick in the Seat of the Pants*. New York: Warner, 1986.

Packard, Vance. *The Pyramid Climbers*. New York: McGraw-Hill, 1962.

Page, Rick. *Hope Is Not a Strategy*. New York: Nautilus Press, 2002.

Pasmore, William. *Designing Effective Organizations: The Sociotechnical Systems Perspective*. New York: Wiley, 1988.

Patterson, Marvin. *Accelerating Innovation: Improving the Processes of Product Development*. New York: Van Nostrand Reinhold, 1993.

Peter, Lawrence J. *The Peter Principle*. New York: William Morrow & Co., 1969.

Peters, Tom. *Liberation Management*. New York: Knopf, 1992.

Peters, Tom. *Thriving on Chaos*. New York: Knopf, 1987.

Peters, Tom. "The WOW Project." *Fast Company* magazine, May 1999.

Peters, Tom, and Bob Waterman. *In Search of Excellence*. New York: HarperCollins, 1982.

Pinto, Jeffrey K. *Power and Politics in Project Management*. Upper Darby, PA: Project Management Institute, 1996.

Pinto, Jeffrey K., Editor. *The Project Management Institute Project Management Handbook*. San Francisco: Jossey-Bass, 1998.

Prahalad, C. K., and Gary Hamel. "The Core Competence of the Corporation." Watertown, MA: *Harvard Business Review*, 1990.

Ray, Michael L., and Rochelle Myers. *Creativity in Business*. Garden City, NY: Doubleday, 1986.

Reinertsen, Donald G. *Managing the Design Factory*. New York: The Free Press, 1997.

Rickards, Tudor. *Problem Solving through Creative Analysis*. Epping, Essex, England: Gower Press, 1975.

Ries, Al. *The 22 Immutable Laws of Branding*. New York: HarperCollins, 2002.

Ries, Al, and Jack Trout. *The 22 Immutable Laws of Marketing*. New York: HarperCollins, 1993.

Rosen, Robert H. *Leading People: The 8 Proven Principles for Success in Business*. New York: Penguin Books, 1996.

Rosenthal, Robert, and Lenore Jacobson. *Pygmalion in the Classroom*. New York: Holt, Rinehart, and Winston, 1968.

Saaty, Thomas L. *Decision Making for Leaders*. Pittsburgh: RWS Publications, 1995.

Sabbagh, Karl. *Twenty-First Century Jet*. New York: Scribner, 1996.

Schuster, John P., Jill Carpenter, and Patricia Kane. *The Power of Open-Book Management*. New York: Wiley, 1996.

Senge, Peter. *The Fifth Discipline*. New York: Doubleday, 1990.

Senge, Peter. Interview in *Fast Company*, May 1999.

Smith, Hyrum W. *The 10 Natural Laws of Successful Time and Life Management*. New York: Warner Books, 1994.

Smith, Preston G., and Donald G. Reinertsen. *Developing Products in Half the Time*. New York: Van Nostrand, 1995.

Stacey, Ralph D. *Complexity and Creativity in Organizations*. San Francisco: Berrett-Koehler, 1996.

Steiner, Claude. *Scripts People Live By*, Second Edition. New York: Grove Weidenfeld, 1990.

Sugimoto, T. *Estimation on the Project Management Workload*. In *Proceedings of the International Conference on Project Management*, Singapore, July 31 to August 2, 2002.

Sykes, Charles. *A Nation of Victims: The Decay of the American Character*. New York: St. Martin's Press, 1992.

Sykes, Charles. *Dumbing Down Our Kids*. New York: St. Martin's Press, 1995.

Treacy, Michael, and Fred Wiersema. *The Discipline of Market Leaders*. Reading, MA: Addison-Wesley, 1995.

Vroom, Victor, and Arthur Jago. *The New Leadership*. Englewood Cliffs, NJ: 1988.

Vroom, Victor, and Phillip Yetton. *Leadership and Decision Making*. Pittsburgh: University of Pittsburgh Press, 1973.

Walpole, Ronald E. *Introduction to Statistics*, Second Edition. New York: Macmillan, 1974.

Watzlawick, Paul, John Weakland, and Richard Fisch. *Change: Principles of Problem Formulation and Problem Resolution*. New York: Norton, 1974.

Weisbord, Marvin. *Productive Workplaces*. San Francisco: Jossey Bass, 1987.

Weisbord, Marvin, Editor. *Discovering Common Ground: How Future Search Conferences Bring People Together to Achieve Breakthrough Innovation, Empowerment, Shared Vision, and Collaborative Action*. San Francisco: Berrett-Koehler, 1992.

Weisbord, Marvin, and Sandra Janoff. *Future Search: An Action Guide to Finding Common Ground in Organizations and Communities*. San Francisco: Berrett-Koehler, 1995.

Wheatley, Margaret. *Leadership and New Science*. San Francisco: Berrett-Koehler, 1992.

White, Gregory L. "In Order to Grow, GM Finds That the Order of the Day Is Cutbacks." *The Wall Street Journal*, 12/18/2000.

Wing, R. L. *The Tao of Power*. New York: Doubleday, 1986.

Wysocki, Robert K. *Effective Project Management*, Second Edition. New York: Wiley, 2000.

Wysocki, Robert K, and James P. Lewis. *The World-Class Project Manager*. Boston: Perseus Books, 2000.

Young, S. David, and Stephen F. O'Byrne. *EVA® and Value-Based Management*. New York: McGraw-Hill, 2001.

Zander, Rosamund Stone, and Benjamin Zander. *The Art of Possibility*. Boston: Harvard Business School Press, 2000.

# INDEX

# ABOUT THE AUTHORS

**James P. Lewis, Ph.D.** is an experienced project manager, who now teaches seminars on the subject throughout the U.S., England, and the Far East. His solid, no-nonsense approach is largely the result of the 15 years he spent in industry, working as an Electrical Engineer, engaged in the design and development of communication equipment. He held various positions, including Project Manager, Product Engineering Manager, and Chief Engineer, for Aerotron, Inc. and ITT Telecommunications, both of Raleigh, NC. He also was a Quality Manager for ITT Telecom, managing a department of 63 quality engineers, line inspectors, and test technicians.

While he was an engineering manager, he began work-ing on a doctorate in organizational psychology, because of his conviction that a manager can only succeed by develop-ing good interpersonal skills.

Since 1980, Dr. Lewis has trained over 30,000 supervi-sors and managers in Argentina, Canada, England, Germany, India, Indonesia, Malaysia, Mexico, Singapore, Sweden, Thai-land, and the United States. He has written articles for *Training and Development Journal, Apparel Industry Magazine,* and *Transportation and Distribution Magazine,* and is the au-thor of *Project Planning, Scheduling and Control, Third Edition, Mastering Project Management, The Project Manager's Desk Ref-erence, Second Edition, Working Together: The 12 Principles Em-ployed by Boeing Commercial Aircraft to Manage Projects, Teams, and the Organization, Project Leadership,* and *The Project Man-ager's Survival Guide,* published by McGraw-Hill, and *Funda-mentals of Project Management, Second Edition; How To Build and Manage a Winning Project Team; and Team-Based Project Management,* published by the American Management Asso-ciation. He is co-author, with Bob Wysocki, of *The World-Class Project Manager,* published by Perseus in 2001. The first edition of *Project Planning, Scheduling and Control* has been published in a Spanish edition, and the AMACOM book *Fundamentals of Project Management* has been published in Portuguese and Latvian. Several of his books have also been published in Chinese, and *Project Leadership* is being trans-lated into Spanish and Russian.

He has a B.S. in Electrical Engineering and a Ph.D. in Psy-chology, both from NC State University in Raleigh. He is a member of the Project Management Institute. He is also a cer-tified Herrmann Brain Dominance Instrument practitioner.

He is president of The Lewis Institute, Inc., a training and consulting company specializing in project management, which he founded in 1981.

Jim is married to the former Lea Ann McDowell, and they live in Vinton, Virginia.

**Louis Wong, MBA** is a Director of Corporate Quality at Creative Technology Ltd, a leading company of Digital Entertainment Products and Services. He is also a Director of Professional Development for Project Management Institute, Singapore Chapter. Before joining Creative, Louis was a Director of Product Improvement Projects for Philips Optical Storage, a division of Royal Philips Electronics of the Netherlands.

Louis was trained in Electronic Engineering and has pursued Quality Management as a profession. He has more than 20 years Quality and project management experience, including various positions with MiniScribe, Maxtor, and National Semiconductor.

He lives in Singapore with his wife, Angelina and 3 children, Leticia, Abraham, and Leo.